**ISSUES THAT CONCERN YOU**

# Juvenile Crime

Heidi Watkins, *Book Editor*

**GREENHAVEN PRESS**
*A part of Gale, Cengage Learning*

GALE
CENGAGE Learning™

Detroit • New York • San Francisco • New Haven, Conn • Waterville, Maine • London

Christine Nasso, *Publisher*
Elizabeth Des Chenes, *Managing Editor*

*For more information, contact:*
Greenhaven Press
27500 Drake Rd.
Farmington Hills, MI 48331-3535
Or you can visit our Internet site at gale.cengage.com

**LIBRARY OF CONGRESS CATALOGING-IN-PUBLICATION DATA**

Juvenile crime / Heidi Watkins, book editor.
    p. cm. -- (Issues that concern you)
 Includes bibliographical references and index.
 ISBN 978-0-7377-4955-7 (hardcover)
 1. Juvenile delinquency--Juvenile literature. I. Watkins, Heidi.
 HV9069.J778 2010
 364.36--dc22
                                                          2010012620

Printed in the United States of America
1 2 3 4 5 6 7 14 13 12 11 10

# CONTENTS

On October 7, 2009, Daija, a thirteen-year-old New York City junior high school student, was harassed by two strangers soon after her mother dropped her off for school. Distressed, she texted her mother. A school safety officer (SSO) observing the situation told Daija to go inside. Daija, however, wanted to wait for her mother outside and refused. The SSO started pulling her into the building, and she resisted. Additional SSOs were called, who dragged her into the school, tripped her to the floor, pinned her to the ground, handcuffed her, and taunted her. Daija was not arrested, but she was injured badly enough to need medical attention. Before this incident, she enjoyed school and wanted to be a veterinarian.

"Lex was here. 2/1/10. . . . I love my friends Abby and Faith,"[1] and a smiley face. Those were the doodles on a school desk in lime green marker that were the basis for the arrest of a twelve-year-old New York City junior high school student in February 2010. Alexa Gonzalez was handcuffed and escorted to the police station, to be released several hours later. The incident landed Alexa in family court, where she was sentenced to eight hours of community service, a book report, and an essay on what she learned from the experience. She was also suspended from school. Her mother says that the situation has been extremely traumatic for the whole family, but especially for Alexa, who has been vomiting from the stress.

## Police in the Schools

What is happening here? In 1998 school safety was handed over to the New York City Police Department, and the principals and teachers no longer really have the authority to handle discipline problems, even the small ones like being late to class, using a cell phone, or talking back. This police force is enormous, with

*At fourteen, Shaquanda Cotton, left, was convicted of assault and served a seven-year sentence. Many thought the sentence was too harsh.*

two hundred armed police and over fifty-two hundred SSOs—a larger police force than in many major cities such as Detroit, Las Vegas, and Dallas.

It does not end in New York City, however. In Paris, Texas, fourteen-year-old high school freshman Shaquanda Cotton was arrested for shoving a hall monitor. In March 2006 she was convicted of "assault on a public servant"[2] and sentenced to prison for up to *seven years*. Shaquanda is African American. Her family was livid, especially when it came to light that the same judge had sentenced a fourteen-year-old Caucasian girl to only three months of probation after she was convicted of arson for burning her family's home down. In 2007, after a public outcry and a scandal involving sexual abuse of incarcerated juveniles in Texas, Shaquanda was released from prison.

Arrests like the ones above, while extreme, should not be disregarded. Studies show that being arrested in school damages kids psychologically. It doubles their odds of eventually dropping out of school and quadruples those chances if a court appearance is involved. It also increases their chances of future police interaction. Furthermore, low-income schools with large Latino and African American populations are the most affected.

## School-to-Prison Pipeline

These anecdotes are not isolated events, but a national trend in public education—a trend toward punishment and zero tolerance and away from nurturing and second chances. This educational trend is part of an even larger trend that experts and activists call the school-to-prison pipeline.

The school-to-prison pipeline refers to the circumstances, policies, and practices that funnel the nation's most at-risk children, particularly minority children and children with learning disabilities, from their classrooms to juvenile and even criminal justice systems. This term, used by groups such as the American Civil Liberties Union (ACLU), and the term "cradle to prison pipeline"[3] used by the Children's Defense Fund (CDF), draw attention to the apparent priority of incarceration over education. In the words of one newspaper journalist, Michelle Chen, writing for *The Juneau Empire*: "Labeled and punished as troublemakers or delinquents, vulnerable children are frequently funneled into a pattern that activists call the 'school-to-prison pipeline.' Expulsion rates suggest that schools are dealing with 'problem' students by simply erasing them. Nationwide, about 3.3 million students were suspended from school in 2006 alone."[4]

According to the ACLU, the stops along the way in the pipeline are "failing public schools, zero-tolerance and other school discipline, policing school hallways, disciplinary alternative schools, and court involvement and juvenile detention."[5] According to the CDF, the pipeline starts earlier, at birth—or even before birth—with "pervasive poverty, inadequate access to health coverage, gaps in childhood development, disparate educational opportunities, intolerable abuse and neglect, unmet mental and emotional problems, and rampant substance abuse."[6]

So, while the handcuffing of a young teen girl at school for doodling on a desk, wanting her mother, or pushing a hall monitor might grab the headlines on any given day, overzealous school policing of minority students is in fact a very small part of the larger issue of the school-to-prison pipeline. Similarly, the school-to-prison pipeline is just one issue within the context of juvenile crime.

Juvenile crime is definitely a complicated issue. Furthermore, it is a significant problem and a matter worthy of discussion by professionals as well as students. The articles in this volume represent multiple viewpoints surrounding the issue. The varied perspectives will enable students to understand the issue more fully, yet also see it in its full complexity.

## Notes

1. Quoted in Rachel Monahan, "Queens Girl Alexa Gonzales Hauled out of School in Handcuffs After Getting Caught Doodling on Desk," *New York Daily News*, February 4, 2010. www.nydailynews.com/ny_local/education/2010/02/05/2010-02-05_cuffed_for_doodling_on_a_desk.html.
2. Bob Herbert, "School to Prison Pipeline," Truthout, June 9, 2007. www.truthout.org/article/ bob-herbert-school-prison-pipeline.
3. Children's Defense Fund, "Cradle to Prison Pipeline Campaign." www.childrensdefense.org/helping-americas-children/cradle-to-prison-pipeline-campaign.
4. Michelle Chen, "'School-to-Prison Pipeline' Must End," *Juneau Empire*, January 28, 2010. www.juneauempire.com/stories/012810/opi_555995206.shtml.
5. American Civil Liberties Union, "Locating the School-to-Prison Pipeline," June 6, 2008. www.aclu.org/files/images/asset_upload_file966_35553.pdf.
6. Children's Defense Fund, "Cradle to Prison Pipeline Campaign."

# ONE

# Juvenile Crime Is Declining

## Charles Puzzanchera

> The Office of Juvenile Justice and Delinquency Prevention (OJJDP), part of the U.S. Department of Justice, publishes several editions of the *Juvenile Justice Bulletin*, each describing training, research, statistics, or programs funded by OJJDP contracts and grants. The edition that makes up this viewpoint, written by Charles Puzzanchera, senior research associate, is part of the Juvenile Justice Data Analysis Project and summarizes statistics from the FBI report *Crime in the United States 2007*. The data reveal a changing trend in juvenile arrests. In 2005 and 2006 arrests had increased slightly, but in 2007 juvenile arrests declined overall by 2 percent, and juvenile arrests for violent crimes declined by 3 percent.

In 2007, law enforcement agencies in the United States made an estimated 2.18 million arrests of persons under age 18. Overall, there were 2% fewer juvenile arrests in 2007 than in 2006, and juvenile violent crime arrests declined 3%, reversing a recent upward trend. Juvenile arrest rates, particularly Violent Crime Index rates, had increased in 2005 and again in 2006 amid fears that the Nation was on the brink of another juvenile crime wave. These latest data show increases in some offense categories but declines in most—with most changes being less than 10% in either direction.

Charles Puzzanchera, "Juvenile Arrests 2007," *Juvenile Justice Bulletin*, Office of Juvenile Justice and Delinquency Prevention, April 2009. Reproduced by permission.

These findings are drawn from data that local law enforcement agencies across the country report to the FBI's Uniform Crime Reporting (UCR) Program. Based on these data, the FBI prepares its annual *Crime in the United States* statistical compilation, which summarizes crimes known to the police and arrests made during the reporting calendar year. This information is used to describe the extent and nature of juvenile crime that comes to the attention of the justice system. Other recent findings from the UCR Program include the following:

- Juveniles accounted for 16% of all violent crime arrests and 26% of all property crime arrests in 2007.
- Juveniles were involved in 12% of all violent crimes cleared in 2007 and 18% of property crimes cleared.
- In 2007, 11% (1,810) of all murder victims were under age 18. More than one-third (35%) of all juvenile murder victims were under age 5, but this proportion varied widely across demographic groups.
- The juvenile murder arrest rate in 2007 was 4.1 arrests per 100,000 juveniles ages 10 through 17. This was 24% more than the 2004 low of 3.3, but 72% less than the 1993 peak of 14.4.
- Between 1998 and 2007, juvenile arrests for aggravated assault decreased more for males than for females (22% vs. 17%). During this period, juvenile male arrests for simple assault declined 4% and female arrests increased 10%.
- In 2007, although black youth accounted for just 17% of the youth population ages 10 through 17, black juveniles were involved in 51% of juvenile Violent Crime Index arrests and 32% of juvenile Property Crime Index arrests.
- The 2007 arrest rates for Violent Crime Index offenses were substantially lower than the rates in the 1994 peak year for every age group under 40.

## In 2007 About One in Ten Murder Victims Were Juveniles

Each *Crime in the United States* report presents estimates of the number of crimes reported to law enforcement agencies. Although many crimes are never reported to law enforcement, murder is one crime that is nearly always reported.

An estimated 16,930 murders were reported to law enforcement agencies in 2007, or 5.6 murders for every 100,000 U.S. residents. The murder rate was essentially constant between 1999 (the year with the fewest murders in the last three decades) and 2007. Prior to 1999, the last year in which the U.S. murder rate was less than 6.0 was 1966.

Of all murder victims in 2007, 89% (or 15,120 victims) were 18 years of age or older. The other 1,810 murder victims were under age 18 (i.e., juveniles). The number of juveniles murdered in 2007 was 9% more than the average number of juveniles murdered in the prior 5-year period, and 37% less than the peak year of 1993, when an estimated 2,880 juveniles were murdered. During the same prior 5-year period, the estimated number of adult murder victims fell 30%.

*Several studies claim that arrests for juvenile crime are declining.*

Of all juveniles murdered in 2007, 35% were under age 5, 69% were male, and 49% were white. Of all juveniles murdered in 2007, 26% of male victims, 53% of female victims, 41% of white victims, and 27% of black victims were under age 5.

In 2007, 68% of all murder victims were killed with a firearm. Adults were more likely to be killed with a firearm (70%) than were juveniles (52%). However, the involvement of a firearm depended greatly on the age of the juvenile victim. In 2007, 17% of murdered juveniles under age 13 were killed with a firearm, compared with 80% of murdered juveniles age 13 or older. The most common method of murdering children under age 5 was by physical assault: In 50% of these murders, offenders' only weapons were their hands and/or feet, compared with only 2% of juvenile victims age 13 or older and 4% of adult victims. In 2007, knives or other cutting instruments were used in 8% of juvenile murders and 13% of adult murders.

## One in Eight Violent Crimes Were Attributed to Juveniles

The relative responsibility of juveniles and adults for crime is difficult to determine. Law enforcement agencies are more likely to clear (or "close") crimes that juveniles commit than those committed by adults. Thus, law enforcement records may overestimate juvenile responsibility for crime.

Data on crimes cleared or closed by arrest or exceptional means show that the proportion of violent crimes cleared and attributed to juveniles has been rather constant in recent years, holding between 12% and 13% from 1996 through 2007. The proportions of both forcible rapes and aggravated assaults attributed to juveniles fluctuated between 11% and 12% over this period, while the proportion of murders ranged between 5% and 6% from 1998 through 2007. In contrast, the proportion of robberies attributed to juveniles varied, falling from 18% to 14% between 1996 and 2002 and then increasing gradually to 17% by 2007.

In 2007, 18% of Property Crime Index offenses cleared by arrest or exceptional means were cleared by the arrest of a juvenile.

This was one percentage point less than the level in 2006; the level in 2007 was the lowest level since at least the mid-1960s. For comparison, the proportion of Property Crime Index offenses that law enforcement attributed to juveniles was 28% in 1980 and 22% in both 1990 and 2000.

## Juvenile Arrests for Violence Declined Between 2006 and 2007

The FBI assesses trends in violent crimes by monitoring four offenses that are consistently reported by law enforcement agencies nationwide. These four crimes—murder and nonnegligent manslaughter, forcible rape, robbery, and aggravated assault—form the Violent Crime Index.

Following 10 years of declines between 1994 and 2004, juvenile arrests for Violent Crime Index offenses increased 11% from 2004 to 2006, then declined 4% through 2007. Given that the number of arrests in 2004 was smaller than in any year since 1987, the number of juvenile Violent Crime Index arrests in 2007 was still relatively low. In fact, the number of juvenile violent crime arrests in 2007 was less than any year in the 1990s, and just 3% greater than the average annual number of such arrests between 2001 and 2006.

The number of juvenile arrests in 2007 for forcible rape was less than in any year since at least 1980, and the number of juvenile aggravated assault arrests in 2007 was less than in any year since 1988. In contrast, after also falling to a relatively low level in 2004, juvenile arrests for murder increased each year from 2005 to 2007. To put it in perspective, if the 2004–2007 increase was to continue annually into the future, it would take another 20 years for the annual number of juvenile murder arrests to return to its peak level of the mid-1990s. However, juvenile arrests for robbery increased more than 30% since 2004. If this pace continues, the annual number of juvenile robbery arrests will return to its 1995 peak in just 4 years. Between 1998 and 2007, the number of arrests in most offense categories declined more for juveniles than for adults.

# Percentage of Arrests Involving Juveniles

In 2007 juveniles were involved in one in ten arrests for murders and about one in four arrests for robbery, burglary, larceny-theft, motor vehicle theft, and weapons violations.

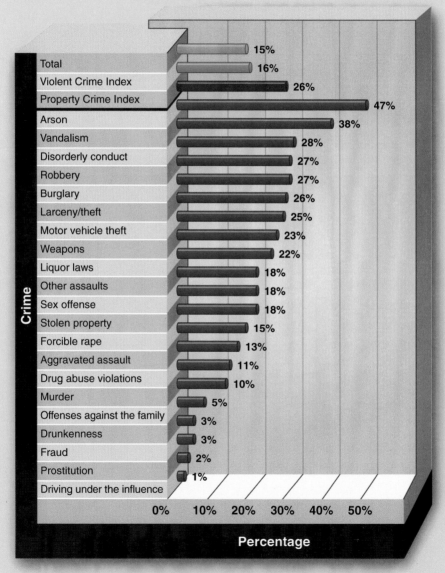

| Crime | Percentage |
|---|---|
| Total | 15% |
| Violent Crime Index | 16% |
| Property Crime Index | 26% |
| Arson | 47% |
| Vandalism | 38% |
| Disorderly conduct | 28% |
| Robbery | 27% |
| Burglary | 27% |
| Larceny/theft | 26% |
| Motor vehicle theft | 25% |
| Weapons | 23% |
| Liquor laws | 22% |
| Other assaults | 18% |
| Sex offense | 18% |
| Stolen property | 18% |
| Forcible rape | 15% |
| Aggravated assault | 13% |
| Drug abuse violations | 11% |
| Murder | 10% |
| Offenses against the family | 5% |
| Drunkenness | 3% |
| Fraud | 3% |
| Prostitution | 2% |
| Driving under the influence | 1% |

Taken from: Charles Puzzanchera, "Juvenile Arrests 2007," *OJJDP Juvenile Justice Bulletin*, April 2009. www.ojp.usdoj.gov.

## Juvenile Property Crime Arrests Increased in 2007—the First Time in Thirteen Years

As with violent crime, the FBI assesses trends in the volume of property crimes by monitoring four offenses that are consistently reported by law enforcement agencies nationwide. These four crimes, which form the Property Crime Index, are burglary, larceny-theft, motor vehicle theft, and arson.

For the period 1980–1994, during which juvenile violent crime arrests increased substantially, juvenile property crime arrests remained relatively constant. After this long period of relative stability, juvenile property crime arrests began to fall. Between 1994 and 2006, the number of juvenile Property Crime Index arrests fell by half to their lowest level since at least the 1970s. However, between 2006 and 2007, the number of juvenile arrests for property crimes increased (up 4%)—for the first time since 1993–1994. This increase was a result of growth in the number of juvenile arrests for larceny-theft, which rose 8% from 2006 to 2007. Juvenile arrests for motor vehicle theft and arson reached historic lows in 2007, while arrests for burglary declined 2% since 2006.

## Most Arrested Juveniles Were Referred to Court

In most States, some persons younger than age 18 are, because of their age or by statutory exclusion, under the jurisdiction of the criminal justice system. For arrested persons under age 18 and under the original jurisdiction of their State's juvenile justice system, the FBI's UCR Program monitors what happens as a result of the arrest. This is the only instance in the UCR Program in which the statistics on arrests coincide with State variations in the legal definition of a juvenile.

In 2007, 19% of arrests involving youth who were eligible in their State for processing in the juvenile justice system were handled within law enforcement agencies and the youth were released, 70% were referred to juvenile court, and 9% were referred directly to criminal court. The others were referred to a welfare agency or to another police agency. In 2007, the proportion of juvenile arrests sent to juvenile court in cities with a population of more than 250,000 (68%) was similar to that in smaller cities (71%).

## In 2007 Females Accounted for 29 Percent of Juvenile Arrests

Law enforcement agencies made 641,000 arrests of females under age 18 in 2007. From 1998 through 2007, arrests of juvenile females decreased less than male arrests in most offense categories (e.g., aggravated assault, burglary, and larceny-theft); in some categories (e.g., simple assault, drug abuse violations, and DUI), female arrests increased, while male arrests decreased.

Gender differences also occurred in the assault arrest trends for adults. Between 1998 and 2007, adult male arrests for aggravated assault fell 12%, while female arrests fell 1%. Similarly, adult male arrests for simple assault fell 6% between 1998 and 2007, while adult female arrests rose 11%. Therefore, the female proportion of arrests grew for both types of assault. It is likely that the disproportionate growth in female assault arrests over this period was related to factors that affected both juveniles and adults.

Gender differences in arrest trends also increased the proportion of arrests involving females in other offense categories for both juveniles and adults. The number of drug abuse violation arrests of juvenile females grew 6% between 1998 and 2007, while juvenile male arrests declined 8%. Drug abuse violation arrests of adult females grew more than adult male arrests (31% and 19%, respectively). The greater decline in male than in female arrests for Property Crime Index offenses seen for juveniles between 1998 and 2007 was also seen in adult arrests, with adult male arrests falling 7% and adult female arrests increasing 9%.

## Juvenile Arrests Disproportionately Involved Minorities

The racial composition of the U.S. juvenile population ages 10–17 in 2007 was 78% white, 17% black, 5% Asian/Pacific Islander, and 1% American Indian. Most juveniles of Hispanic ethnicity were included in the white racial category. Of all juvenile arrests for violent crimes in 2007, 47% involved white youth, 51% involved black youth, 1% involved Asian youth, and 1% involved American Indian youth. For property crime arrests, the proportions were 66% white youth, 32% black youth, 1% Asian youth, and 1% American Indian youth. Black youth were overrepresented in juvenile arrests.

The Violent Crime Index arrest rate (i.e., arrests per 100,000 juveniles in the racial group) in 2007 for black juveniles (903) was about 5 times the rates for white juveniles (180) and American Indian juveniles (183) and 16 times the rate for Asian juveniles (57). For Property Crime Index arrests, the rate for black juveniles (2,453) was more than double the rates for white juveniles (1,081) and American Indian juveniles (1,147) and more than 6 times the rate for Asian juveniles (371).

In the 1980s, the Violent Crime Index arrest rate for black juveniles was between 6 and 7 times the white rate. This ratio declined during the 1990s, falling to 4-to-1 in 1999. Between 1999 and 2007, the racial disparity in the rates increased, reaching 5-to-1 in 2007. This increase resulted from an increase in the black rate (5%) and a decline in the white rate (25%). More specifically, the robbery arrest rate increased 37% for black juveniles while the white rate declined 17%, and the aggravated assault rate declined less for black (12%) than for white juveniles (27%).

# TWO

# Urban Gun Violence Is an Increasing Part of Juvenile Crime

## John Buntin

> In 2007, 134 murders occurred in Cleveland, Ohio, an increase of 56 percent from 2004. Similar increases were seen during this period in other large cities. In this viewpoint John Buntin, a staff writer covering crime and urban affairs for *Governing* magazine, looks at the rising murder rate, its connection to the prevalence of guns, and some controversial measures that some cities are taking to combat it. In Cleveland and Philadelphia, police initiatives employing stop-and-frisk measures are targeting high-crime neighborhoods in an attempt to control rising gun violence. The measures are controversial because they would not be tolerated in other neighborhoods, but they have been supported by a 1968 court decision.

Every day, a kid is brought in—head hung, wrists cuffed behind his (or, occasionally, her) back, a police officer on each arm, steering the offender into the small holding room in the basement of Cleveland's Juvenile Detention Center. These are Cuyahoga County's most dangerous—and most troubled—youth. The mother beaters. The school brawlers charged with aggravated assault. The "slingers" caught with crack cocaine on the corner.

John Buntin, "Gundemic: After a Decade of Declining Crime, Urban Gun Violence Is Surging Again. Police Are Being Told to Get Tough," *Governing*, June 2008. Reproduced by permission.

Three years ago [in 2005], charges of drug possession and trafficking were what brought many, if not most, of these kids here. Not anymore. To all intents and purposes, says Sam Amata, the head of the juvenile division in the Cuyahoga County public defender's office, the drug charges "have gone away." It's almost always firearms now. The most notorious recent cases—five teenagers who terrorized a Shaker Heights lawyer out for a jog on New Year's Eve; a 15-year-old robber who shot a convenience store clerk and then demanded cash from him; the 17-year-old pulled out of the wreck of a stolen car with a bullet-proof vest strapped to his body—all involved guns.

The city of Cleveland is awash in guns. Some are legal, thanks to Ohio's lenient concealed-weapons law. Many are not. Either way, they are ending up in the hands of young men who are willing to use them. The result, says Mayor Frank Jackson, has been "a lethal combination" that's driven the homicide rate up to levels that haven't been seen in more than a decade.

## A Rise in Urban Violence

Since 2004, Cleveland's murder rate has risen by 56 percent from 86 in 2004 to 134 in 2007. Cleveland's experience is not unique. After a decade during which violent crime fell across the country by 30 percent, violent crime in general—and gun crime in particular—has returned to many American cities. Since 2005, Atlanta, Baltimore, Detroit, Miami and Philadelphia have seen alarming increases in homicide. The trend is not yet a national one: In the first half of 2007 (the most recent period for which data are available), nationwide violent crime rates were essentially flat. But many big cities have been hit hard. The worst numbers, says University of Pennsylvania criminologist Lawrence Sherman, are in cities with highly concentrated, racially segregated poverty, lax gun laws, and relatively few of the immigrant newcomers who seem to make dangerous areas safer.

However, even cities that have so far avoided homicide spikes are worried. Earlier this year [2008], Los Angeles and New

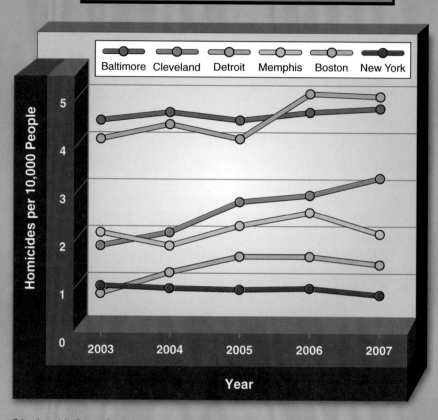

## Homicides per 10,000 People

Baltimore  Cleveland  Detroit  Memphis  Boston  New York

Homicides per 10,000 People

Year

Taken from: John Buntin, "Gundemic: After a Decade of Declining Crime, Urban Gun Violence Is Surging Again. Police Are Being Told to Get Tough," *Governing*, June 2008, p. 27.

York, long considered national models for falling crime, saw sharp and worrisome homicide increases. Equally ominous, homicide clearance rates are falling in most of the country—meaning that more people are getting away with murder.

Faced with this bad news, police departments have been focusing their attention on guns. In Baltimore, gun offenders are now required to keep police informed of where they live. In Boston (which saw sharp increases in homicide in 2005) and in Washington, D.C. (which experienced 7 percent more homicides last year than in 2006), police have begun to send officers into high-crime neighborhoods to ask parents for permission to search their kids' rooms for illegal firearms (with the understanding that any guns found will be moved, with no charges filed).

But Cleveland and Philadelphia have gone further. In both cities, African-American mayors have directed their police departments to use tactics in high-crime, black neighborhoods that few white mayors would dare to authorize. In Philadelphia, Mayor Michael Nutter has instructed police to conduct more "stop-and-frisk" searches. In Cleveland, Mayor Jackson signed off in January [2008] on an aggressive new gun-suppression strategy that hinges on profiling pedestrians who might be carrying guns. If it is successful, it could redefine the boundaries of what is considered acceptable in policing. If it fails, it could inflame the very tensions that Jackson has spent much of his life trying to alleviate. The mayor puts it bluntly, "I say to people, 'Don't call the pit bull out and tell it not to bite.'" . . .

## The Controversial "Stop and Frisk"

Targeting guns is not new. The first and perhaps most successful example of a police department using this strategy occurred in Kansas City in 1992 and '93. The department there selected two demographically similar districts. In one, police practices were left unchanged. The other district received additional patrol units, which focused on stopping cars and searching them for weapons. The results were impressive. Over the course of six months, gun crimes in the targeted area fell by nearly 50 percent from the level of the previous six months, and homicides declined, as well. In the other area, gun crimes increased. In the years that followed, a handful of other jurisdictions tried similar tactics, with generally encouraging results.

The Kansas City police, however, were targeting people in automobiles. The Cleveland police have chosen to do something trickier—target individuals on the street. In doing so, they have come face to face with one of the most common—and most controversial—tactics in policing: "stop and frisk."

The history of this approach is complicated. Until the late 1960s, police departments enjoyed sweeping powers to stop and search pedestrians they suspected of potential criminal involvement. In 1968, in a case called *Terry v. Ohio*, the U.S. Supreme Court changed the rules somewhat.

The case concerned a Cleveland detective, Martin McFadden, who observed three men apparently casing out a store in the neighborhood. McFadden confronted the men, identified himself as a police officer, and asked for their names. When their response was unclear, he spun one of the men around and patted

*Cleveland mayor Frank Jackson, center, has directed his police force to pursue an aggressive strategy of profiling possible gun-toting pedestrians in predominately black neighborhoods.*

down his outside clothing. He felt a revolver. He patted down a second man and found another gun. All three were booked for illegally carrying concealed weapons.

The defense argued that these actions amounted to an unconstitutional search and seizure. The Supreme Court disagreed, in a departure from its series of rulings favoring criminal suspects and limiting police authority, and sided with Detective McFadden. "Where a reasonably prudent officer is warranted in the circumstances of a given case in believing that his safety or that of others is endangered," Chief Justice Earl Warren wrote, "he may make a reasonable search for weapons of the person believed by him to be armed and dangerous." So McFadden's approach was given legal sanction as a method of crime control—although with some modest restrictions.

Ever since, "stop and frisk" has become a deeply resented tactic in African-American neighborhoods around the country. The fact that it now is being relied on heavily by black mayors such as Jackson and Nutter—Nutter campaigned in favor of it and won easily—is a testament to frustration with the sudden rise in urban violence.

Some experts have sought to temper the notion that an aggressive and questionable expansion of police powers is underway. "I don't like the word 'aggressive,'" says Sherman. As he sees it, the Philadelphia police department is merely making "a systematic effort to put specially trained police in the places at the times where and when gun violence is more likely to occur. . . . The police need to be very thorough in observing people on the street who may be carrying guns because it is well known that people in that particular location can and do use illegally carried guns to shoot people." . . .

## On the Street

The Fourth District is a good place to take the measure of what Cleveland's police are up to. Southeast of downtown, the Fourth encompasses some of the city's toughest neighborhoods, just as it did in the days when [Cleveland police chief Michael]

McGrath patrolled it. As a result, the department's gun-suppression teams conduct frequent operations in the district.

When gun-suppression or narcotics units are not working the area, responsibility for proactive policing falls largely to the Fourth District vice squad. A nighttime operation in mid-April [2008] offered insights into how the new strategy works—and into the limitations.

The department doesn't allow media ride-alongs with the gun-suppression teams. It says the work is simply too dangerous. But it did allow *Governing* to observe another important part of the city's anti-gun strategy—the first evening of a three-night, neighborhood safety initiative. Where gun-suppression teams focus on looking for weapons (although they also make drug arrests), the neighborhood safety initiatives have a broader purpose —bringing zero-tolerance, quality-of-life policing to dangerous and often chaotic neighborhoods.

At City Hall or in the downtown Justice Center, these neighborhood safety initiatives are described as a three-day blitz against all forms of criminal activity. In the Fourth District, on upper Kinsman Road, this would seem an impossible task. To the extent that the neighborhood has a functional economy, it is largely an underground and illicit one. The officers who patrol it know that the streets flanking Kinsman Road are full of establishments that could legally be busted—the grill that's "a notorious weed spot," the smoke shop that until recently openly advertised drug paraphernalia, the biker hangout-turned-illegal "after hours" club. But there are simply too many to shut down, even for a night or two.

As the evening progresses, it becomes clear that Mayor Jackson's new strategies have changed some things in important ways. At its most basic level, the initiative means more officers are on the street. In an area such as this, where just two months earlier a uniformed patrol officer was killed after he attempted to question a group of youths drinking in an abandoned building, that's very important indeed. Fewer suspects get away. Officers feel emboldened to be more assertive. They look harder for guns.

It's just after 10 o'clock on a rainy Thursday night. The vice squad already has been out for about two hours with a planted, confidential informant, doing drug "buy and busts"—and also looking for illegal guns to take off the street. Thanks to the weather, it's been a quiet night. Only one gunshot has been heard. Over the course of two hours, the vice squad has made two arrests. They are over quickly. Plainclothes officers with binoculars and radios ("the eyes") stake out the corner where the informant—known as "the property" or "the package"—is making the buy, usually a $20 rock of crack cocaine. (The informant is paid $25 per buy and is usually good for six or seven buys before he is considered to be "burned out.")

Once the deal is made, plainclothes and uniformed officers move in for the arrest. The suspect usually tries to run. Most of the time, he is caught. This evening, one suspect gets away with $20 in taxpayer funds, leaving the supervising officer deeply annoyed. Another location doesn't pan out: The police arrive and quickly stop, frisk and cuff two men. One has $700 in cash but no drugs. He claims to be a contractor. The cuffs are removed. The police informant later says the deals were occurring inside the house, which the police can't raid without a warrant.

Then, with buy number five, the vice squad hits the jackpot. The police are staking out a dealer on the corner of Kinsman and East 143rd Street when their radio crackles. There is a drug dealer there with what is reported to be a rifle. The tension subsides a little when the stakeout officer radios in a correction —it's a paintball gun.

The police move in to make the arrest. By the time the supervising sergeant and lieutenant arrive on the scene, the dealer is spread-eagled against a wall—and a revolver is being removed from the back of his pants. One dealer has just learned a hard lesson about carrying a handgun. That, says Chief McGrath, is the point.

Only one gun is seized on the first night of this particular neighborhood safety initiative. The gun-suppression teams, however, have been more successful. In the first four-and-a-half months of 2008, the Cleveland Police Department sent out 104 gun-suppression teams—basically, one a day. The teams made 287 arrests and confiscated 55 illegal firearms. There have been no reported complaints. On the contrary, says Mayor Jackson, constituents are asking, "When is it coming this way?"

The police department is confident the program is working. "Compared to the same period in 2007, homicides for the first quarter of 2008 are down 33 percent," says Chief McGrath.

In short, the view from the downtown Justice Center is pretty optimistic right now. Still, out on the street, the numbers aren't all so rosy. Two numbers from the paintball gun arrest make it clear just how difficult Cleveland's struggle against gun violence is likely to be. The paintball gun cost about $160. Anybody who wanted a revolver could get one on Kinsman Road for $65.

Guns are still everywhere on the streets of Cleveland.

# THREE

# Gang Violence Involving Girls Is Increasing

Nancy Macdonald

> In recent years crimes committed by juvenile girls have increased by an estimated 25 percent in the United Kingdom, and the incarceration of women has increased by 11 percent in Canada, reports Nancy Macdonald for *Maclean's*, a weekly Canadian newsmagazine. Furthermore, it seems that for the first time, women are being targeted for murder by gangs, which goes against a traditional street culture taboo. In this viewpoint Macdonald examines the rising involvement of girls in crime, especially gang-related crime. She discusses their motivations for joining gangs, how their involvement differs from that of their male counterparts, and how they are victimized by male gangs.

First came the shooting death of Brianna Kinnear. On Feb. 3 [2009], the pretty, blond, 22-year-old crack-cocaine dealer was found slumped over the steering wheel of a black Dodge pickup in Coquitlam, B.C. [British Columbia]. It had "all the hallmarks of a targeted murder," say police. So did the shooting death, two weeks later, of Nikkie Alemy, 23, a young mom with ties to the UN gang, who was gunned down in a silver Cadillac in a busy Surrey intersection. Then, last month [May 2009], 36-year-old Laura Lamoureux was found shot to death in a Langley gutter. Known to police for her involvement in the street-level drug trade, her death, too, bore the "signature" of a "targeted murder," say police.

Their murders are "precedent-setting," says gang expert Cathy Prowse: in 15 years of research, the University of Calgary criminal sociologist has never seen a gang-related, targeted shooting of a woman in Canada. Until now, "the code of the street said you didn't take out women," says Prowse. But that code runs two ways: women have also avoided involvement in drug distribution—and stepping on the "economic turf of rivals." Now, with so many young women "getting caught up in the game," says Charysse, 21, who exited a Scarborough, Ont. [Ontario], gang last year, "the code" no longer applies.

## More Women in Jail

Recent research shows female gang membership and women's involvement in criminal activities are on the rise in Canada and beyond. Girls—who are also closing the gender gap in terms of drug use and abuse—are no longer just appendages to male gangs: some are forming gangs of their own. Whereas the number of Canadian males behind bars decreased by nine per cent between 2002 and 2007, the number of women jumped by 11 per cent, according to a new report by Statistics Canada. In the U.K., crimes committed by young women have soared by 25 per cent in the past three years. (Of London's 174 gangs, police estimate at least three are exclusively female.) And last year, evidence emerged showing women may account for as much as 40 per cent of Central America's fierce street gangs, including Mara Salvatrucha.

## An All-Girl Gang

Canada-wide, six per cent of gang members are thought to be female, ranging from a low of three per cent in Ontario to a high of 12 per cent in B.C., according to a study by Canadian gang expert Michael Chettleburgh. But because police traditionally

## Ten-Year Juvenile Arrest Trends, 1998–2007

**Percentage change in arrests in the United States, 1998–2007:**

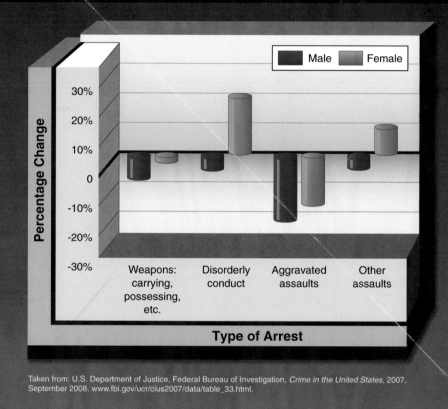

Taken from: U.S. Department of Justice, Federal Bureau of Investigation, *Crime in the United States*, 2007, September 2008. www.fbi.gov/ucr/cius2007/data/table_33.html.

under-arrest females, he believes those figures are grossly understated; he thinks the true number is closer to a third, adding that Canada recently welcomed its first all-female gang. The Indian Posse Girls—an auxiliary to the Winnipeg-based Indian Posse gang—are thought to control Edmonton's sex trade.

Women have an easier time recruiting girls into this work, he says. Female gang members carrying product or weapons can also fly under police radar, says Charysse. Whereas a group of males might have "records or priors"—giving police a pretty clear idea of what they might be up to—"the attention's not on us," she says. Anatomy helps too, says Tammy, who, starting at

16, logged 10 years in two Prairie street gangs, before quitting Edmonton's Redd Alert gang after her recent release from prison for a gang-related robbery. It's too risky for men to carry drugs in their pockets: they risk getting jumped, or stopped by police. Women, who are less likely to be frisked by police, can hide the drugs in their body and ferry it to the point of sale, she says.

Charysse—whose brother and ex-boyfriend were part of the same gang—says girls now also help run debit- and credit-card scams in banks and clothing stores. Gangs are increasingly earning money through electronic fraud, says Sgt. Shinder Kirk of B.C.'s integrated gang task force. Police believe women with clean criminal records are being deployed by gangs to work in banking and insurance corporations. But none of this is new, argues U.S. criminologist Meda Chesney-Lind, who studies female delinquency. She says much research on gangs has simply ignored females or trivialized female gangs.

## Girls Are Less Violent

U.S. research shows that TV gangster girls notwithstanding— Snoop, on HBO's *The Wire*, is crueller than many of her male colleagues—female gang members commit fewer violent crimes, and are more inclined to property crimes and drug offences. That may be tied to the fact that women are seldom involved in the upper levels of gangs, according to Chicago criminologist John Hagedorn. He says a lot of girls are "terribly" sexually exploited within mixed-sex gangs—another reason to view females and gangs as a serious social concern. Girls tend to act as escorts, prostitutes, drivers, and intelligence-gatherers, says Charysse, whose role included "sex object." Pretending to be "some guy's girl," she would find out "where he lived, how much money he made, or what spots he dealt from."

## Gangs as a Refuge

Some women do earn power by association. Tammy's ex-boyfriend was one of Redd Alert's "top dogs." She "sold dope

*The author reports that although female gang members commit fewer violent crimes than their male counterparts, they are more likely to commit property and drug crimes.*

and beat up people if they owed money," and for a brief period, had the fur coat, the "family," and the cash, but left because she grew tired of doing time. Tammy says girls join for the same reason guys do: "to be noticed, to feel part of something." But research shows they are "much, much" more likely to join a gang as a refuge from "really bad situations at home, including incest," says Joan Moore, one of the first U.S. criminologists to study gangster girls. She wrote *Going Down to the Barrio*, which details the lives of L.A.'s Chicana gangsters. In 1994, Moore found 29 per cent of L.A. gang members had reported sexual abuse at home; Chesney-Lind's 1995 follow-up study put the figure closer to two-thirds.

In the end, most, for better or worse, fall prey to the "mommy track," says Hagedorn. Charysse, who joined in Grade 9, exited at 20, shortly after the birth of her child. "I got arrested, and I just stepped back, and was like: okay, if I end up doing time, and my daughter's father is in jail, she doesn't have anybody." Soon after, she left her boyfriend, and turned her back on gang life, working two jobs to support her daughter, whom she is now raising alone. "That was not the life I wanted for her," she says.

# FOUR

# Violence in Girls Is Not Increasing but Still Warrants Special Attention

Margaret A. Zahn, Stephanie R. Hawkins, Janet Chiancone, and Ariel Whitworth

The Office of Juvenile Justice and Delinquency Prevention (OJJDP), part of the U.S. Department of Justice, started the Girls Study Group in 2004, bringing experts together to develop a better understanding of the causes and solutions for delinquency in girls. After reviewing more than two thousand journal articles and book chapters, the group published a summary of their findings to date in a report prepared by Margaret A. Zahn, principal scientist at Research Triangle Institute (RTI) International; Stephanie R. Hawkins, research clinical psychologist with RTI International; Janet Chiancone, research coordinator at OJJDP; and Ariel Whitworth, a communications editor with the National Crime Justice Reference Service. This viewpoint contains excerpts from that report and includes risk factors for delinquency, factors that protect against delinquency, and the developmental sequence of delinquent behavior in girls. While the group found that girls are not more violent than in previous years, more girls are entering the juvenile justice system. The group calls for

Margaret A. Zahn, Stephanie R. Hawkins, Janet Chiancone, and Ariel Whitworth, "Girls Study Group: Understanding and Responding to Girls' Delinquency," Office of Juvenile Justice and Delinquency, October 2008. Reproduced by permission.

more work with law enforcement to develop programs and systems to mediate community and family conflict.

Juvenile delinquency can become a pathway to adult offending. Delinquency experts search for ways to counter delinquency before it starts, providing intervention for juveniles in high-risk situations—such as those with severe economic disadvantages or living in high-crime neighborhoods.

However, the majority of juveniles arrested are male, which means that a good deal of research on juvenile delinquents has been performed on a mostly male population that does not account for girls' and boys' differences. Despite much research on the causes of boys' delinquency, few studies have examined which girls become delinquent or why. Additionally, intervention and treatment programs have been traditionally designed with boys in mind, and little is known about how well girls respond to these interventions.

In the 1990s, a surge of girls' arrests brought female juvenile crimes to the country's attention. Girls' rates of arrest for some crimes increased faster than boys' rates of arrest. By 2004, girls accounted for 30 percent of all juvenile arrests, but delinquency experts did not know whether these trends reflected changes in girls' behavior or changes in arrest patterns. The juvenile justice field was struggling to understand how best to respond to the needs of the girls entering the system.

To determine the reason behind these increasing arrest rates, the Office of Juvenile Justice and Delinquency Prevention (OJJDP) convened the Girls Study Group. The group sponsored a series of studies to gain a better understanding of girls' involvement in delinquency and guide the development, testing, and dissemination of strategies that would reduce incidents of delinquency and violence among girls.

The Girls Study Group (GSG) wanted to know—
- Which girls become delinquent?
- What factors protect girls from delinquency?
- What factors put girls at risk for delinquency?
- What pathways lead to girls' delinquency?

- What programs are most effective in preventing girls' delinquency?
- How should the criminal justice system respond to girls' delinquency? . . .

## Violence by Teenage Girls: Trends and Context

The upswing in girls' violence in the late 20th century had many people in the juvenile justice community concerned. They wanted to know what factors influenced girls' offending, and what kinds of programs and policies could reduce girls' violence.

To answer these questions, OJJDP convened the Girls Study Group. The Group's initial research project examined rates of girls' arrests, delinquency, and victimization. Researchers examined

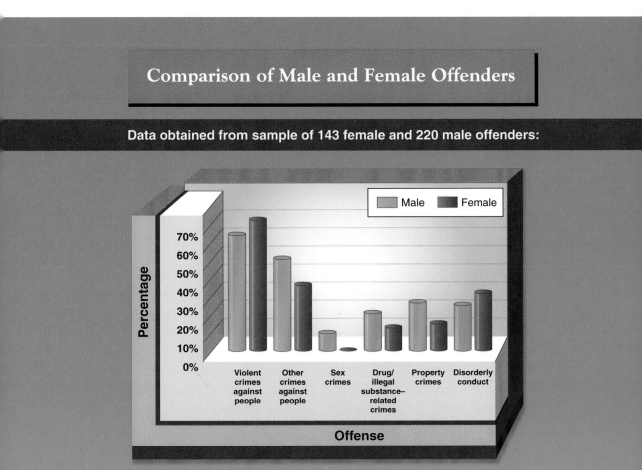

### Comparison of Male and Female Offenders

Data obtained from sample of 143 female and 220 male offenders:

Taken from: Don Martin et al., "Profile of Incarcerated Juveniles: Comparison of Male and Female Offenders," *Adolescence*, Fall 2008.

arrest data from the FBI's Uniform Crime Reports, delinquency surveys from the Monitoring the Future study, and victimization surveys from the Bureau of Justice Statistics' National Crime Victimization Survey.

This research resulted in the *Trends and Context* Bulletin, which provides answers to a number of questions:

*How have girls' and boys' arrest rates increased in the past decade?*

- Girls account for a smaller proportion of overall juvenile arrests than boys, but arrest patterns for both groups have diverged over the past decade. Between 1996 and 2005, overall arrests decreased for both groups. However, this decrease was greater for boys than girls.
- Notably, between 1996 and 2005, girls' arrests for simple assault increased 24 percent.

*Are girls actually committing more crimes?*

- Despite increasing arrest rates in the past decade, self-report data suggest that girls' behavior has not changed. In fact, self-report data suggest girls' and boys' assault rates have dropped in recent years.

*What would explain the increasing arrest rates for girls?*

Arrest laws and changes in law enforcement policy appear to have had more of an impact on arrest rates than changes in girls' behavior. Possible explanations for this include:

- Changes in local law enforcement policies that lowered the threshold for reporting assaults or classifying assaults as aggravated.
- Some status offenses involving a domestic dispute between a girl and her parent or sibling could now be classified as simple assault and could result in arrest. This sort of arrest is an unintended consequence of "mandatory arrest" laws in cases of domestic violence.
- Schools' zero-tolerance policies toward youth violence may have increased police referral for fights involving girls.

To test some of the possible explanations outlined above, the Girls Study Group conducted a special analysis that looked at local mandatory and pro-arrest policies to determine if there were indications that these had an impact on the increasing number of girls' arrests. Their findings indicate that mandatory and pro-arrest policies increased the likelihood of arrest for both girls and boys, but the effects appear stronger for girls. This may be explained by the fact that family conflict accounts for a larger proportion of girls' offending than of boys' offending.

## Causes and Correlates of Girls' Delinquency

Girls' delinquency has become an increasing dilemma in recent years, in part because of higher arrest rates, and in part because little research to date has focused on female juvenile delinquents. By 2004, females made up 25 percent of all juvenile arrests for aggravated assault, and 33 percent of juvenile arrests for other assaults. So why do some girls become delinquent? A great deal of research has examined the factors involved in male delinquency, but the factors involved in female delinquency remained largely unknown.

To understand the causes of female delinquency, the Girls Study Group reviewed more than 2,300 social science articles and book chapters that examine factors involved in delinquent behavior for girls ages 11 to 18. They also examined factors that protect girls from becoming delinquent. They found that while certain factors predict or prevent delinquency in both sexes, a number of factors influence girls' behavior more strongly than boys' behavior.

The factors that equally increase the risk of delinquency for both sexes include—

- The family's dynamics (i.e., how parents supervise and monitor a child, family history of criminal behavior, child maltreatment).
- A child's involvement in school.
- The neighborhood a child lives in (e.g., poverty level, crime rate, employment rate).
- The level of availability of community-based programs.

Some factors increase or decrease a girl's risk of delinquency more than a boy's, including—

- *Early puberty*. Early puberty increases girls' risk for delinquency, particularly if they come from disadvantaged neighborhoods and have dysfunctional families. This disparity between biological and social maturity can lead to increased conflict with parents or negative associations with older boys or men.
- *Sexual abuse or maltreatment*. Compared to boys, girls experience more sexual victimization overall, including sexual assaults, rapes, and sexual harassment. However, all types of maltreatment (sexual, physical, and neglect) can increase the risk of delinquency for both sexes.

*Girls who experience such factors as early puberty, sexual abuse, depression, and anxiety have a greater risk of delinquency than do boys.*

- *Depression and anxiety.* Depression and anxiety disorders have been associated with delinquency. Girls receive these diagnoses more frequently than boys.
- *Romantic partners.* When a youth's boyfriend or girlfriend commits a crime, he or she may also engage in delinquent behavior. For less serious crimes, girls are influenced more by their boyfriends than boys by their girlfriends. For serious crimes, they are equally affected.

## Resilient Girls—Factors That Protect Against Delinquency

Some children manage to achieve success despite the difficulties they encounter in life. This ability to positively adapt to negative situations is called resilience. Positive experiences in life can strengthen a child's ability to become resilient to the difficult situations—abuse, neglect, poverty, witnessing violence—that can lead to delinquency.

An investigation by the Girls Study Group examined whether experiencing protective factors during adolescence could keep girls from offending. These protective factors included—
- Support from a caring adult.
- Success in school—as measured by grade point average.
- School connectedness—a positive perception of the school environment and positive interactions with people at school.
- Religiosity—how important religion was to the girl.

The researchers analyzed self-report surveys from the National Longitudinal Study of Adolescent Health. They found:
- *Caring adult.* Girls who had a caring adult in their lives during adolescence were less likely to commit status or property offenses, sell drugs, join gangs, or commit simple or aggravated assault during adolescence. They also were less likely to commit simple assault as young adults.
- *School connectedness.* Girls who experienced school connectedness were not protected or at increased risk for delinquency during adolescence and young adulthood,

with one exception—girls who experienced school connectedness during adolescence were more likely to become involved in aggravated assault in young adulthood.

- *School success.* Girls who experienced success in school during adolescence committed fewer status and property offenses and were less likely to join gangs in adolescence. School success helped protect them from involvement in simple and aggravated assault in adolescence and young adulthood. However, these girls were more likely to commit property offenses in young adulthood.
- *Religiosity.* Girls who placed a high importance on religion during adolescence were less likely to sell drugs in early adolescence.

Researchers additionally examined the interaction between childhood risk factors and protective factors during adolescence on a child's propensity toward delinquent behavior. Although some of the protective factors helped girls not to engage in delinquent behavior, others could not mitigate the influence of risk factors that girls had endured since childhood. Their findings highlight the importance of considering girls' life histories when developing interventions for girls at high risk for delinquency. . . .

## Developmental Sequences of Girls' Delinquent Behavior

As girls develop, their experiences and interactions impact their decisions and behavior. Some of these experiences and interactions may contribute to positive developmental outcomes and others may support involvement in negative behaviors.

The Girls Study Group explored the possibility that distinct developmental pathways could influence girls' delinquent behaviors. The resulting Bulletin may help researchers develop programs or policies that stop female delinquency before it starts.

To investigate the developmental pathways that lead to delinquency, the Girls Study Group analyzed data from two longitudinal studies of girls between ages 7 and 17—the Denver

Youth Study, which included 807 girls and the Fast Track Project, which included 317 girls. The authors examined the lifetime prevalence of the types of delinquent behaviors [in which] girls were involved, including running away, truancy, public disorderliness, minor assault, minor property offense, serious property offense, serious assault, drug sales, alcohol use, and drug use; and the developmental sequences of delinquent behavior followed by different groups of girls over the 7–17 age period.

The authors found that girls followed different developmental sequences. No one sequence or pathway of delinquent behaviors applied to a majority of girls. Additionally, a sizable proportion of girls were involved in delinquent offenses before middle school. Girls involved in more serious offending tended to return to a lower level of status or public disorder offending or returned to a nondelinquent status after a short time.

## Girls Are Not More Violent than in Previous Years

The research conducted by the Girls Study Group has yielded very important information for OJJDP and the juvenile justice field. Some of the findings have confirmed earlier research and anecdotal information, while other findings have contradicted many of the long-held beliefs about how girls become delinquent and how best to address their needs.

One of the first findings—and in some ways the most surprising finding—is that girls are not more violent than in previous years. The comparative analysis of official FBI data to self-report data revealed that, in fact, a change in how the juvenile justice system is responding to girls' behavior is largely responsible for the increased number of girls entering the system. Another surprising finding is that the increase in girls' arrests appears to be, in part, an unintended result of relatively new mandatory or pro-arrest policies put in place to protect victims of domestic violence. These are good policies, and necessary to protect victims. However, this unexpected outcome highlights the need to work with law enforcement to identify appropriate responses to conflict between girls and their family members, and for communities to support and provide families with access to family strengthening and mediation programs that provide intervention (rather than arrest).

## Shared Risk Factors

Another key finding of the study group is that girls and boys experience many of the same delinquency risk factors. Although some risk factors are more gender sensitive, in general, focusing on general risk and protective factors for all youth seems a worthwhile effort. When it comes to providing intervention programming, some unique factors should be considered for girls. As with all delinquency prevention and intervention efforts, however, the focus should be on the individual youth and her specific needs and strengths. This is why using the appropriate risk assessment tools is important, whether the youth is a girl or a boy. . . .

In moving ahead, the Girls Study Group findings will provide OJJDP with the foundation needed to move ahead on a comprehensive program of information dissemination, training, technical assistance, and programming regarding girls' delinquency prevention and intervention. The findings of the group may assist States and communities in developing their own efforts to address girls' delinquency.

# FIVE

# Potential Juvenile Offenders Should Receive Early Intervention

## Christine Siegfried

Teenagers are more than twice as likely as adults to be victims of nonfatal violent crimes. Many teens are resilient and recover with few aftereffects. Some do not. According to many experts, one of the possible effects of victimization is violence and juvenile delinquency. In this viewpoint Christine Siegfried, network liaison for the National Center for Child Traumatic Stress, explores the relationship between victimization and violence, writing for *The Prevention Researcher*. She explains possible theories for the relationship as well as strategies for preventing these negative outcomes of victimization, such as early intervention, improved reporting, interventions through schools, and publicizing the victim compensation that is already available.

A dolescent victimization is common. In fact, teenagers experience rates of violent crime far higher than other age groups. For example, a recent report from the U.S. Department of Justice showed that on average youth aged 12–17 were about

2.5 times as likely as adults to be the victim of a nonfatal violent crime. They were twice as likely to be robbery or aggravated assault victims, 2.5 times as likely to be victims of a rape or sexual assault, and almost 3 times as likely to be victims of a simple assault. The National Survey of Adolescents found that 13% of girls and 3.4% of boys reported being sexually assaulted at some point in their lives. The same survey reported that 21.3% of boys and 13.4% of girls experienced physical assault, and 43.6% of boys and 35% of girls reported having witnessed violence at some time in their lives.

## Profile of Incarcerated Juveniles: History of Abuse

**Data is by percentage of sample of 143 female and 220 male offenders**

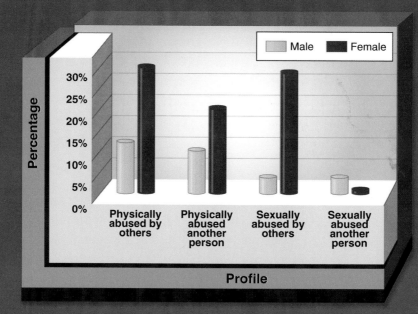

Taken from: Don Martin et al., "Profile on Incarcerated Juveniles: Comparison of Male and Female Offenders," *Adolescence*, Fall 2008.

While most adolescents survive victimization with relatively few adverse consequences, victimization can disrupt the course of child development in fundamental ways and can contribute to problems over the course of a life span. Studies have shown a clear relationship between youth victimization and problems later in life, including mental health problems, substance abuse, impaired social relationships, victimization as an adult, and suicide. There also appears to be a significant relationship between victimization and later delinquency and perpetration of violence. For example, both the National Survey of Adolescents and the Adolescent Health Survey showed that victimized youth were much more likely to be juvenile offenders than their nonvictimized peers, and the difference was especially notable for violent offenders. While most professionals agree that no single risk factor or experience leads a young person to delinquency, the chances of offending increase when a teenager is a witness to or victim of violence and experiences traumatic stress as a result. This article will explore the relationship between adolescent victimization and subsequent violence, then explores ways to prevent violence by preventing victimization and intervening with those who have been victimized.

## The Relationship Between Victimization and Violence

Researchers have suggested different explanations for the relationship between victimization and violence. Some point out that violent victimization and violent offending share many of the same risk factors, such as drug or alcohol use. Others note that victims and victimizers often have similar social, situational and environmental characteristics and lifestyles, such as living in areas with high crime rates. Social learning theory suggests that violence may be learned through experiencing it or observing it and that it may be transmitted from one generation to the next in a "cycle of violence."

Many researchers believe trauma and posttraumatic stress disorder (PTSD) symptoms to be an explanatory or contributing

*Social learning theory suggests that violence is learned through experience and can be perpetuated from generation to generation.*

factor to the development of aggressive behavior. Fear, high arousal, and hypervigilance experienced by traumatized youth may lead them to misinterpret the behavior of others as hostile or threatening and respond with aggression. Youth who feel that society cannot protect them may develop aggressive or violent methods to protect themselves.

A number of strategies have been identified which may short-circuit this cycle of victimization and subsequent violence. These strategies, which include prevention and intervention approaches, are outlined below.

## Target Interventions to Those Groups Most Likely to Be Victimized

Clearly some groups are at higher risk than others for violent victimization. Many, but not all, studies have found that youth who are poor, African American, Hispanic or American Indian are at the highest risk for victimization. Researchers have found that youth who live in single-parent families, urban areas, disadvantaged communities, and families who have recently moved into the community are more likely to be victimized.

Additionally, children with physical, emotional, or developmental disabilities or needs are particularly vulnerable to victimization. Homeless adolescents are vulnerable to victimization and are at increased risk of being harmed the longer they are on the streets. Gay youth and those perceived to be gay are also at higher risk for victimization, bullying and harassment. Prevention efforts, public education efforts, and early intervention efforts are best targeted to these groups that are at highest risk for victimization.

## Improve Reporting of Youth Victimization

Most youth victimizations, including serious violent victimizations such as aggravated assault and rape, are not reported to police or other authorities. If crimes are not reported, teenage victims have less opportunity to access support and services that might help them recover from the trauma.

Contributing factors for not reporting may include adolescent concerns about personal autonomy, fears of being blamed or not taken seriously, fears of retaliation, or fears of being punished for engaging in risk-taking behavior or associating with deviant peers. Additionally, families may be concerned about involving their children in the justice system, and youth and adults may not perceive the offenses against youth as real crimes.

Shock, shame, and stigma also frequently accompany victimization and are reasons youth may not want to report victimization. Youth, especially boys, may also feel that they were weak and should have been able to defend themselves. If the victimization was committed by an acquaintance or another youth, the victim may feel reluctant to turn in that person to police. Teens who have been victimized are often convinced that they are different or "not normal." If they have been assaulted by somebody of the same sex, they may wonder if they will be seen as gay or if the event will "make them gay." Teenagers may be particularly reluctant to disclose some types of victimizations in front of their parents or families. Gay youth have additional barriers to reporting—fear of outing themselves and the possibility that the person they report to is homophobic or nonresponsive. These youth need messages about their right to safety and acceptance.

In order to improve reporting of youth victimization, the justice system needs to emphasize its interest in assisting juvenile victims, remove the disincentives to reporting, train and deploy staff members who specialize in youth victimization, and make staff more available and accessible where youth gather. Police and school officials should talk openly about victimizations of children as serious criminal acts.

Communities likewise need to provide incentives to report incidents, including information to help youth protect themselves from future victimization or from retaliation. Public education and outreach campaigns can help educate parents and their children about what constitutes a crime, what victims may feel, the importance of reporting victimization, and places to go to get help and be safe. Some teens who don't want to report right away will need this type of information later.

## Reach Out to Already Victimized Teens

Teens who have been victimized once are at risk for being victimized again. For this reason, all public education materials and programs should include information for those already victimized. Outreach materials should be made available in places where teens gather (schools, recreation programs, theaters, malls). Some outreach materials should be placed where a teen can take down a number or pick up a flier privately (restrooms, fitting rooms, the Internet).

Intervention models need to be designed for youth without traditional family, school or service system support. Outreach workers need to be on the streets talking to teenagers who are runaways, homeless or involved with the juvenile justice system in order to build trust. One promising program is the intimate partner violence prevention program offered by the Hollywood Homeless Youth Partnership in Los Angeles. This program is designed to increase the skills of homeless youth in resisting and responding to interpersonal violence. It is delivered in shelters and drop-in youth agencies.

## Intervene Early with Teen Victims

Given that there is some evidence to suggest that offending and subsequent victimization occur fairly soon following violent victimization, interventions may be most successful in preventing future offending and victimization if they are applied relatively soon after the initial victimization. Victimized children need to be identified quickly and their continued safety ensured. They need to be able to communicate what happened and to have their experience validated. They need emotional support from non-offending family members, their caretakers, the school, and professionals. Traumatic reaction to victimization can also be minimized when assistance is provided quickly.

Many youth are reluctant to talk about their victimization. So professionals and youth workers may need to specifically ask youth whose behavior has become troubling, "What's going on?"

## Screen Youth in Substance Abuse and Delinquency Programs

Studies report 70–90% of youth in the juvenile justice system have been exposed to traumatic events, either as victims or as witnesses, and as a result many have developed PTSD or other stress-related disorders. Research also indicates that there is a strong connection between interpersonal violence and a risk of substance abuse or dependency. In fact, there is some evidence to suggest that some forms of interpersonal violence may heighten the risk for having both a substance abuse problem and [a] mental health disorder. Given the connection between victimization and both substance abuse and delinquency, adolescent alcohol and drug use programs and juvenile justice programs should screen youth entering for a history of violent assault and witnessing violence.

Juvenile justice and substance abuse programs also need to be alert for events that unintentionally retraumatize young people in their settings. Arrest and detention experiences, along with being housed together with older or more violent adolescents, have exposed some teenagers to risks for additional victimization and trauma.

## Strengthen School Interventions

Schools play a significant role in delivering mental health interventions to youth. Many also play a role in responding to and preventing youth victimization. Universal school-based interventions, such as The Fourth R, are being used to teach adolescents skills to combat relationship violence. This comprehensive school program uses best practice approaches to target multiple forms of interpersonal violence. Other school-based programs, such as Second Step by the Committee for Children, teach younger students social emotional skills to reduce aggressive and impulsive behavior. Some schools implement programs that emphasize respect and tolerance for diversity and reduce tolerance for bullying. More primary prevention programs are needed.

For certain families, schools appear to play a major role in getting mental health services to children, especially to children whose parents may not have thought about getting services for their child. School counseling services are critical, but still lacking in many schools. Offering school-based services reduces stigma and allows young people to use services without drawing attention to themselves.

Safe Horizon, a nonprofit organization in New York City, runs a Safe Harbor program in New York schools. This program combines victim assistance, trauma education, violence prevention, individual counseling, parent involvement, structured group activities and a school-wide anti-violence campaign. Evaluations of Safe Harbor supported the use of a victim assistance model as a way to effectively prevent violence among youth.

Children who are expelled from school are at increased risk for victimization. Schools need to have a variety of ways of intervening with troubled youth. "No tolerance" policies and automatic expulsions often end up stripping teens of their last vestiges of protection and supervision and propel them into unsafe communities. The availability of after school programs and positive group activities for children still attending school are also vitally important, since adolescents are most likely to be victimized between 3 and 6 P.M.

## Publicize Crime Compensation Funds for Young Victims

Crime victim compensation is available to cover crime-related medical expenses, funeral and burial costs, mental health counseling, and lost wages or loss of support. Victims may also receive funds to replace eyeglasses, for dental services and devices, prosthetic devices and crime scene cleanup. Victims of crime programs provide supportive services and sometimes court accompaniment. Communities need to do more to publicize the availability of crime compensation funds and supportive services for adolescent victims. They also need to expedite and simplify the processing of crime compensation awards for teens. Having representatives from victim assistance programs readily available in key locations that serve teen victims to answer questions and assist is also important.

## Refer Youth and Families for Help

Most adolescent victims of assaults, even those most negatively impacted, do not receive counseling. Yet good, evidence-based trauma-focused interventions exist for adolescents. Cognitive behavioral therapy has been shown to be particularly effective for youth in the juvenile justice system, as well as for youth with more general anger and disruptive behaviors. Cognitive behavioral approaches have proved successful as well in addressing trauma from victimization, along with interventions that emphasize emotion identification and regulation, anxiety management, alteration of maladaptive thoughts, and social problem solving.

The most effective interventions for both victimized teens and juvenile offenders have strong family components. In fact, getting help for families of teens may be critical to the teen's recovery. When family members themselves are also victims of trauma or suffer from depression or anxiety related to the victimization of their teen, therapeutic intervention for the family members may strengthen their capacity to help meet their child's needs as well.

Being victimized increases the likelihood of committing later offenses and engaging in aggressive and violent behavior. It also increases the likelihood of being victimized again. More can be done to interrupt this cycle and ensure the safe and successful transition from adolescence to adulthood. Protecting youth against violent victimization of all types needs to be a priority for community leaders, policy makers and professionals. Along with preventing future problems like substance abuse, suicide and mental health problems, reducing rates of victimization and responding early to young victims to offset the adverse consequences of victimization may actually lessen the severity of juvenile violence and crime in society as a whole.

# SIX

# Many Juvenile Offenders Need Longer Sentences in Juvenile Facilities

Julie Bykowicz

> *Baltimore Sun* reporter Julie Bykowicz draws attention to what she deems are significant deficiencies in the juvenile justice system. She argues that the system is inadequate to deal with the crimes that have become all too common among teenagers: drug dealing, gangland-style murder, rape, armed robbery, violent carjacking, and the like. She points to the recidivism rate of youth offenders as evidence that the system is unequal to today's challenges. Judges should be given the freedom to impose harsher sentences, she maintains, sentencing teenagers as adults when the severity of their crimes warrants and creating sentences that transition with the offender from youth into adulthood.

At 17, Lamont Davis has been arrested 15 times since age 10, including charges of drug dealing, carjacking with a handgun and assaults. Yet he's spent just a handful of weeks in juvenile treatment facilities over the years and was sent home in July [2009] after admitting to charges in a robbery.

Days later, the Baltimore teen was arrested on charges that he critically wounded a 5-year-old girl as he shot at another youth.

That Davis now faces more serious criminal charges than ever, city prosecutors and some public officials say, highlights a dangerous problem in the juvenile justice system: Because it emphasizes rehabilitation over punishment, teens who are lightly sanctioned for early offenses sometimes graduate to more violent crimes. Some, including the city's top prosecutor, are calling for better ways to deal with young offenders, including charging more of them as adults and lengthening the time they can spend in custody or under supervision.

"There are some kids who have exhausted all of the resources that the juvenile system offers," said Baltimore State's Attorney Patricia C. Jessamy. "There are some young people who are not capable of being rehabilitated in the juvenile system, and we need to find another way to deal with those people. Community programs and short detentions is not addressing the issue."

## A Call for Change

The statistics, prosecutors say, bear out what they see in court every day: More than half of the juveniles who return to their communities after the most serious sanction available in juvenile court—an out-of-home placement—are in handcuffs again within a year, according to state data. Three-quarters of them have been rearrested within three years.

"The total process needs to be changed on all levels," Baltimore Mayor Sheila Dixon said in a recent interview. "The number of young people involved in violent crime has increased. It has escalated to the point where it's gotten all of us at the table to better collaborate."

Last year [2008], about 4,200 Baltimore youths faced juvenile charges. Of the ones found responsible for crimes, about 1,100 were removed from their homes to locked facilities, structured foster care and other places. Another 2,300 received services in the community, through programs such as family therapy and electronic home monitoring, or were supervised informally.

## Juveniles Need Different Treatment

Officials at the Maryland Department of Juvenile Services, which oversees young offenders at facilities and in their communities, counter that the system—though not always perfect—is working.

"Do I think that we need to be concerned that juvenile offenders are not being held accountable? No. They are being held accountable. We have 1,200 locked up today [statewide]," said Juvenile Services Secretary Donald W. DeVore. "Generally, if you compare the juvenile system and what's available to help kids, there's no suggestion we would be better off by sending them to the adult system."

DeVore, juvenile experts and public defenders point to research showing that young people have brains different from adults and should be treated differently when they commit crimes. To punish them like adults can have unintended consequences, they say.

A juvenile who serves time in an adult prison will be schooled by more experienced criminals and hardened by what studies show is the harsh treatment they receive there. Some studies show as much as a 100 percent rearrest rate for juveniles who are released from adult prisons.

"The most punitive approach might not get us the most public safety," said Tracy Velazquez, executive director of the Justice Police Institute in Washington. "The adult system does not have age-appropriate resources."

## An Outdated Juvenile System

But prosecutors say young offenders often don't receive the kinds of sanctions that will change their behavior.

Assistant State's Attorney Jennifer Rallo, a juvenile prosecutor for five years, gave several examples of sentences that horrified her. There was the young drug dealer sent home to his 23-year-old sister after he admitted to repeatedly shooting an addict who'd backed out of a buy. He was quickly arrested again for selling drugs. There was the boy who got a brief stint in reform

*Many argue that some juveniles, because of the severity of their crimes, should be tried as adults.*

school after using a gun to hold a family hostage in a home invasion. Within a year after returning home, he'd been arrested four times on drug charges.

Maryland's juvenile system, Rallo said, "was not created for the types of offenders we're seeing today."

The law guiding when juveniles are treated as adults is 40 years old and hasn't been amended in 15 years. Fourteen-year-olds accused of first-degree murder, rape or sex offense and 16-year-olds charged with most other violent crimes are automatically charged as adults, though defense attorneys can—and often do—persuade judges to move their clients to juvenile court.

Prosecutors have urged a reluctant state legislature to add more crimes, particularly gang-related assaults and drug dealing, to the list of offenses for which a teen is charged as an adult.

Jessamy said she wants state lawmakers to consider even broader reforms, including creating a youthful-offender facility in the adult system or "blended sentencing," which would enable judges to sentence violent youths to a juvenile facility until age 18 and then move them into the adult system to serve additional time.

Another blended sentencing option would give Circuit Court judges the power to sentence a young offender to juvenile facilities but with a suspended adult prison term to be served if the youth fails to reform. Though such sentencing is not spelled out in a state law, some Maryland judges have occasionally crafted such sentences.

About half the states have laws enabling one or both kinds of blended sentencing, according to the National Center for Juvenile Justice in Pittsburgh. Yet researchers there say no substantive studies have been done on whether blended sentencing decreases recidivism.

## Lengthened Sentences May Be the Key

A better alternative, Velazquez said, would be to lengthen the time offenders can stay in juvenile facilities. Maryland law says offenders must leave juvenile facilities when they turn 21, though most are released at age 18. Several states, including Oregon, allow judges to sentence youths to juvenile facilities until they are 25.

"The research shows that kids age out of delinquent behavior by then," she said. "If they stay in the juvenile system longer, they're more likely to get the treatment and services they need to improve the chances that they won't re-offend."

DeVore said his agency is on the right path, pointing to increased availability of proven programs like intensive, in-home family therapy. The department, in partnership with the city, also created the Violence Prevention Initiative, which closely supervises about 200 offenders, including teens responsible for robberies and assaults, in the community, checking on them as often as five times a week.

## Better Supervision May Be the Key

Gov. Martin O'Malley said recently that changes in Juvenile Services have "all been about putting a much higher level of supervision and a tighter level of supervision on those people who are on the streets that we know are at risk to themselves or to others."

To public defenders in the Juvenile Protection Division, a group that tracks the services youths receive after sentencing, the juvenile system works well in its current form—if judges, caseworkers and attorneys take the time to find the right treatment for each offender.

When such care is taken, they say, success stories emerge.

Antonio Franklin, a 21-year-old with developmental disabilities and bipolar disorder, works full time as a security guard at Fort Meade and lives in a Catonsville apartment run by a private mental health care provider. He hasn't been in trouble in years and, through his church, serves as a mentor to misbehaving kids.

Five years ago, when Bea Zipperlee, a licensed clinical social worker with the public defender's office, met the Salisbury native, he was in full restraints in a Towson hospital's psychiatric ward. He had tried to kill himself by bashing his head against a wall at an Eastern Shore youth lockup, where he was confined after beating someone with a baseball bat.

Zipperlee, part of the Juvenile Protection Division, persuaded a judge to transfer Franklin from juvenile lockup to Rosewood Center, where he was treated for a year. Then she got him

## States' Use of Private Facilities, 2006

About one-third of juvenile offenders are held in privately operated facilities, but this number varies greatly by state.

| | Percentage of juvenile offenders held in | |
| --- | --- | --- |
| | Public Facilities | Private Facilities |
| **States with Greatest Use of Private Facilities** | | |
| Pennsylvania | 28 | 72 |
| Arkansas | 31 | 69 |
| Iowa | 35 | 65 |
| Wyoming | 37 | 63 |
| Florida | 38 | 62 |
| Massachusetts | 40 | 60 |
| North Dakota | 44 | 56 |
| Michigan | 46 | 54 |
| Alabama | 47 | 53 |
| South Dakota | 47 | 53 |
| **States with Least Use of Private Facilities** | | |
| Maine | 90 | 10 |
| California | 90 | 10 |
| Illinois | 91 | 9 |
| Ohio | 92 | 8 |
| Mississippi | 93 | 7 |
| New Jersey | 93 | 7 |
| New Mexico | 94 | 6 |
| Nevada | 96 | 4 |
| Washington | 96 | 4 |
| Virginia | 98 | 2 |
| Missouri | 99 | 1 |

Taken from: *Office of Juvenile Justice and Delinquency Prevention Statistical Briefing Book*, released on September 12, 2008. Data sources: Office of Juvenile Justice and Delinquency Prevention/Census of Juveniles in Residential Placement, 2006. Washington, DC: OJJDP.

into a private program where he lives alone in an apartment but has around-the-clock access to a caseworker.

"Without the juvenile system, I don't think I would have made it in society," Franklin said. He credits Zipperlee with saving his life. "She would always call me, even after I cussed her out. She always cared about what happened to me. I'd never had that support before."

## Some Juveniles Fall Through the Cracks

Not all offenders find such a watchful advocate as they hurtle through the juvenile system.

That might have been the case with Lamont Davis, who after years of juvenile offenses faces charges as an adult for attempted first-degree murder in the shooting of 5-year-old Raven Wyatt.

According to people with access to his confidential juvenile record, Davis was not placed in a juvenile facility for treatment until 2008. He ran away from two group homes. Then he landed at Mount Clare, a small group home near his Southwest Baltimore neighborhood, where he spent six weeks.

Three workers there, who did not want to be named because of the privacy issue, said he was doing well. "We saw real progress," one employee said. "It was a structured environment, and he seemed to appreciate that structure."

But then Juvenile Services suddenly closed Mount Clare at the end of March [2009], part of what DeVore said was a broader effort to reduce the number of group homes in favor of other programs.

Unable to complete his treatment at Mount Clare, Davis was moved briefly to a shelter. Then he returned home.


## Ideas for Reform:

- Add more categories of crime, particularly gang and drug offenses, to automatic adult jurisdiction.
- Allow juvenile judges to sentence offenders to a juvenile facility until age 18 and then switch them to the adult system to serve additional prison time.
- Persuade Circuit Court judges to sentence teens to juvenile facilities but with an adult prison term hanging over their heads if they fail.
- Extend from 21 to 25 the age at which offenders must leave juvenile facilities.
- Better analyze the needs of new offenders to get them into programs that can truly rehabilitate them.

## When Is a Juvenile Charged As an Adult?

Age 14 and older:

- First-degree murder
- First-degree rape
- First-degree sex offense
- Attempt or conspiracy to commit any of above
- 16- and 17-year-olds charged with first-degree murder cannot be transferred to juvenile court

Age 16 and older:

- Armed robbery
- Attempted armed robbery
- Carjacking (armed and unarmed)
- Second-degree murder
- Attempted second-degree murder
- Second-degree rape
- Second-degree sex offense
- Attempted second-degree sex offense
- Various handgun crimes, including minor in possession

# SEVEN

# Some Juvenile Detention Centers Rely Too Much on Force

Irene Jay Liu

Irene Jay Liu, a contributor for National Public Radio's *Talk of the Nation* and *All Things Considered*, as well as a writer for *The Albany (NY) Times-Union*, writes about investigations into the juvenile criminal justice system by the U.S. Department of Justice, Human Rights Watch, and the American Civil Liberties Union. Investigators found that physical force was utilized all too often—and in extreme measure—while mental health services were underused. While workers in the juvenile system have been criticized by members of these watchdog groups for their mistreatment of the youths in their charge, the workers raise concerns for their own physical safety, citing the ability of young adults to inflict considerable damage to workers.

Children at four of New York's juvenile detention centers—including the Tryon Residential Center in Johnstown—have faced excessive force and lack of proper mental health treatment in violation of their constitutional rights, according to a report by the U.S. Department of Justice released Monday [August 24, 2009].

The report details how staff at the four facilities—Tryon's two facilities, one for boys and one for girls, as well as the Lansing

Residential Center and the Louis Gossett Jr. Residential Center in Lansing, Tompkins County—have routinely used "uncontrolled, unsafe applications of force" to gain control in every type of situation, departing from "generally accepted standards" as well as policies outlined by the state Office of Children and Family Services (OCFS).

"Anything from sneaking an extra cookie to initiating a fist fight may result in a full prone restraint with handcuffs," according to the report.

## Severe Injuries Reported

The report said the excessive use of force has led to an "alarming" number of serious injuries, including concussions, broken or knocked-out teeth, broken bones and spinal fractures.

The report also details numerous incidents of "inappropriate" restraints.

At Tryon, residents described a technique called the "hook and trip," in which staff would hold a youth's arms, then trip them so they fell face first to the ground. Staff would also hold a youth's arms behind their back and then pull up, causing severe pain.

The report said facilities inadequately investigated and disciplined staff for using excessive force.

A staff member was accused of calling a youth a sexual epithet and throwing him to the ground, causing a cut on the chin that required stitches. The employee had a record of force violations, including fracturing a youth's shoulder. The facility recommended termination, but the union negotiated a settlement of a letter of reprimand, an $800 fine and the threat of a two-week suspension if another incident occurred within a year.

## Lack of Mental Health Treatment Reported

The report also found the state failed to provide adequate mental health treatment to children in the four centers and that residents with documented mental health issues were restrained more often than others, especially at Tryon.

"It's nice to see the police toughening up on juvenile crime"

"It's nice to see the police toughening up on juvenile crime," cartoon by Adey Bryant. www.CartoonStock.com.

Fifty percent of the boys at the Tryon facility have some mental illness; they were involved in 82 percent of restraint incidents. At the Tryon girls' facility, 48 percent of the population had mental illness; they were involved in 60 percent of restraint incidents.

The report said one mentally ill youth was restrained eight times during a two-month period, usually for actions the report described as "exhibiting symptoms of her illness," such as banging her head, putting paper clips into her mouth or tying a string around her neck.

The report arose from an investigation initiated on Dec. 14, 2007 in response to allegations of sexual misconduct and excessive use of restraints. The report found no current systemic deficiencies in the area of sexual misconduct.

*New York State's juvenile detention facilities and its Office of Children and Family Services have come under fire for alleged abuses of juveniles in the system.*

## An Extreme Case

A 2006 report by Human Rights Watch and the American Civil Liberties Union, which investigate conditions in juvenile facilities in the United States and around the world, called OCFS "among the most hostile juvenile justice agencies we have ever encountered."

Later that year, 15-year-old Darryl Thompson died after he was pinned face-down by two staff members at Tryon. The Nov. 16, 2006, incident was ruled a homicide but a grand jury did not indict the staff members involved.

Responding to the Department of Justice's report Monday, OCFS Commissioner Gladys Carrion acknowledged long-standing issues, saying that she "inherited a juvenile justice system rife with substantial systemic problems."

Carrion was appointed by former Gov. Eliot Spitzer to head the agency in January 2007 and took steps to convert the juvenile detention system from a "custody and control" model to a "trauma-informed therapeutic model."

Carrion has tangled with public employee unions and elected officials over the swift policy changes, particularly the move to reduce the use of physical restraints.

Last August [2008], Tryon staff member Charles Loftly suffered a stroke after being assaulted by a resident, dying a few days later. Unions faulted Carrion's policy changes.

## A Complex Situation

"These are streetwise kids, many of whom are in for very serious crimes," said Darcy Wells, a spokeswoman for the Public Employees Federation, last August. "They know the staff has been told to reduce the numbers of restraints. And that's increasing the assaults (on staff members) almost daily." In response, the agency temporarily downsized the Fulton County facility, to provide staff members with more training.

Carrion has moved to shut upstate centers in favor of building more community-based programs in New York City, where most of the children in OCFS custody are from, but has met fierce resistance by public employee unions and Senate Republicans who fear job losses in their districts.

In a statement, the Civil Service Employees Association said it "has long had concerns about OCFS operations" but could say no more without additional information.

The Justice Department gave OCFS 49 days to respond with a plan to comply with the report's recommendations.

The report noted the agency's cooperation so far, but said if a resolution can't be reached, the department could move toward a federal takeover of the state's juvenile detention system.

# EIGHT

# Incarceration Is Not the Answer for Juvenile Offenders with Behavioral Health Disorders

Diana Mahoney

> A writer who specializes in health and wellness, Diana Mahoney highlights attempts by some within the juvenile justice system to address the emotional and mental disorders afflicting half to three-quarters of all young people in the system. The focus of the juvenile system has always been rehabilitation rather than incarceration; therefore, measures to address mental health need shoring up. Rather than creating new protocols, gleaning the best approaches from the past and using them in tandem with each other has had tremendous success, not to mention that the cost savings of providing mental health services rather than incarcerating young people are significant.

When it comes to juvenile offenders, the wheels of justice often spin out of sync with community mental health needs and services.

About 50%–75% of incarcerated youth nationwide suffer from a mental or emotional disorder, compared to the estimated 18%–22% of the U.S. youth population as a whole, according to the Coalition for Juvenile Justice (CJJ), a non-profit advocacy organization.

Despite those numbers, the juvenile detention centers and secure-care facilities to which these young people are sent are largely ill equipped to diagnose and treat mental illness. And because many of the behaviors that land young people in detention are linked to undiagnosed and untreated mental health problems, a large percentage of youth become repeat offenders in a cycle that can last throughout adolescence and into adulthood.

These youth are legally entitled to mental health services, but access is limited: An overwhelmed juvenile justice system, ever-changing reimbursement policies, confusion about consent and confidentiality issues, no continuity of care across placement changes, and a lack of treatment-based diversion programs and evidence-based mental healthcare services are among the barriers to effective care faced by juvenile offenders and their families.

## Recommended Change in Focus

Recent policy recommendations for juvenile justice reform from national organizations such as the CJJ and the American Academy of Child and Adolescent Psychiatry have suggested that the juvenile justice system—which is meant to be rehabilitative rather than punitive—shift its focus to the mental health needs of young offenders.

The challenge put forth by these and other organizations is to identify children at risk and implement a comprehensive treatment plan that addresses the individual needs of each child. Toward that end, one management model that has shown evidence-based promise is multi-systemic therapy (MST).

MST, developed by the Family Services Research Center at the Medical University of South Carolina, Charleston, by Scott W. Henggeler, Ph.D., and his colleagues, is more of an amalgam of proven approaches than a wholly new one. It is delivered in

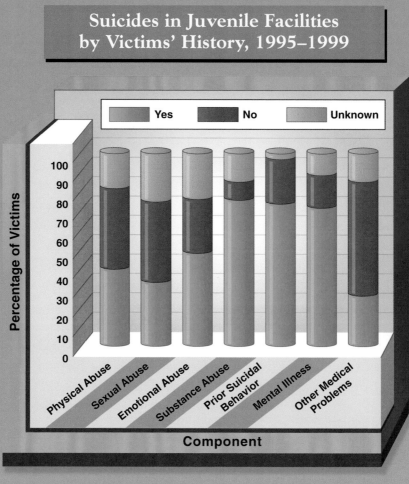

## Suicides in Juvenile Facilities by Victims' History, 1995–1999

Taken from: Jeff Slawikowski, "Characteristics of Juvenile Suicide Confinement," *Office of Juvenile Justice and Delinquency Prevention Juvenile Justice Bulletin*, February 2009. www.ojp.usdoj.gov.

the youths' natural environment (home, school, community), under the premise that children are affected by a complex network of family, peer, and community influences. The only way young offenders and their families will achieve and sustain improvements is to target factors that contribute to their delinquent behaviors and teach them how to function more effectively within that network, Dr. Henggeler said.

"If the goal is to increase the chances that a kid is going to become a productive citizen and decrease the chances that he's going to be involved in crime and drugs, our perspective is that you take mental health resources and devote them to building a positive environment around him," he said.

An MST program typically involves several hours of contact with a therapist per week for 4–6 months. Depending on the youth, the therapy might focus on troubling characteristics of the young person's behavior, the family's disciplinary practices, school performance issues, and/or interaction with deviant peers. Intervention strategies include structural and strategic family therapy, behavioral parent training, and cognitive-behavioral therapies.

## Positive Results

Several controlled studies of MST with serious juvenile offenders have demonstrated long-term reductions in criminal activity, drug-related arrests, violent offenses, and incarceration. Outcome studies by Charles M. Borduin, Ph.D., and Dr. Henggeler showed that 4 years after treatment, 26% of MST youths had been arrested, compared with 71% of the non-MST youths.

Among the youths arrested after treatment, those who received MST were arrested for significantly fewer serious and violent crimes than were their non-MST counterparts.

In addition to the perceived social benefits of MST, the approach appears to be cost effective over the long term, because the incremental costs of the program are usually offset by savings in the usual cost of out-of-home placement as well as those incurred through re-arrests and convictions.

A 1997 evaluation of an MST program in Simpsonville, S.C., showed that despite its intensity, the treatment model was a relatively inexpensive intervention. With a client-to-therapist ratio of 4:1 and a course of treatment lasting 3 months, the cost per client for treatment in the MST group was about $3,500, compared with the then-average cost of institutional placement in South Carolina of $17,769 per offender.

MST Services, affiliated with the Medical University of South Carolina and the Family Services Research Center through an exclusive license agreement, supports communities interested in MST program development.

*Multi-systemic therapy, which includes counseling in the youth's natural environment, has been shown to be effective in helping many young offenders avoid repeated criminal behavior.*

## MST in Practice: A Rural Experiment

Most MST programs have been implemented in urban and suburban settings. But one of the most ambitious implementations can be seen in the Rural Appalachia Project, a community development model aimed at reducing the social and economic costs of juvenile delinquency in rural areas.

Funded by the National Institute of Mental Health, the 5-year study began last summer [2004] and will ultimately include

720 children with serious conduct and other mental health problems who have been referred to juvenile courts in eight poor, sparsely populated counties in the rural Appalachian mountains of eastern Tennessee. To date, more than 100 youth have been recruited—all of whom are at risk of being removed from their homes and placed into state custody.

"We're focusing on the least-populated, poorest counties, where the number of kids in the juvenile justice system and in state custody is disproportionately high," said Charles A. Glisson, Ph.D., director of the Children's Mental Health Services Research Center at the University of Tennessee and the study's lead investigator.

Dr. Glisson said that the number of single parents in these areas is large and that the rate of mental health problems among those parents is high. "These families have very few resources, and once kids are placed in state custody, they are there longer [compared with urban and suburban youth]," Dr. Glisson explained.

## A Focus on Help at Home

The goal of the Rural Appalachia Project is to push the existing infrastructure to provide services in rural areas. "For many of these families, transportation is a problem, and the stigma of mental health services also keeps them from seeking help," he said. "Delivering services to the home as intensely and as frequently as needed addresses both of these issues."

As they are recruited, the young people aged 9–17 are evaluated and randomized to receive either MST or usual care in the community. Therapists are available to the families 24 hours a day, 7 days a week, as needed.

The MST is being implemented on two levels, Dr. Glisson said. On one, an MST-trained therapist works with the child and his or her family in the home. On another, psychologists trained in organizational development run advisory groups in some of the participating counties. "The idea is to establish an infrastructure that can support this new intervention, not only for the period of the study but long alter the study ends," Dr.

Glisson said. This involves educating judges, school administrators, and community leaders about MST.

The program is still too new to have preliminary outcome data, he said. As the project gathers steam, the investigators will evaluate the impact of MST on the mental health of the youth, the psychosocial functioning of the families, recidivism rates, and comparative service costs.

# NINE

# An Adult Life Sentence Without Parole Is Appropriate for Some Juvenile Offenders

Matthew T. Mangino

> Matthew T. Mangino, a writer for the *Pennsylvania Law Weekly* and once a prosecutor for Lawrence County, Pennsylvania, writes about the necessity for courts and judges to have the ability to impose on some juvenile offenders sentences of life in prison without the possibility of parole. In recent years there has been a proliferation of teen criminals who commit extremely violent and heinous crimes and yet show no remorse. Traditional sentencing does not address this frighteningly violent trend Mangino says. And while life without the possibility of parole might be too harsh a sentence for nonviolent offenders, the legal system needs multiple sentencing options in order to address the wide spectrum of youth criminals.

Only days into the new year [2008] a 12-year-old Florida boy was arrested for the murder of his 17-month-old cousin. He beat the toddler to death with a baseball bat. The boy told police the victim, a little girl, was making noise while he watched a cartoon on television.

If the state's attorney had decided to charge the boy as an adult and he was convicted of first-degree murder the court would have been required to impose a sentence of life in prison without the possibility of parole (LWOP). Although the boy was not charged with first-degree murder, the prospect of a 12-year-old boy being sentenced to LWOP has rekindled the debate about sentencing juveniles as adults.

Life without parole is not unlike the death penalty. Paul Wright, a former lifer, told the *New York Times*, "It's a death sentence by incarceration. You're trading a slow form of death for a faster one." Only three years ago [2005] the U.S. Supreme Court banned the execution of juveniles. The decision in *Roper v. Simmons* resulted in the commutation of 72 juvenile death penalties; a significant majority of those juveniles on death row were re-sentenced to LWOP.

In the last several months [the winter of 2007–2008], articles in the *New York Times*, *Chicago Tribune*, and *Detroit Free Press* have written about halting the practice of sending juveniles to prison for life with no hope of parole. The *USA Today* recently published an op-ed calling for reform in sentencing juveniles. With mounting public pressure, policy makers would do well to proceed with caution.

## An Increase in Life Sentences

The surge in juvenile LWOP sentences is a relatively new phenomenon. Prior to 1980, juveniles sentenced to LWOP were extremely rare. As violent crime rates soared in the 1980's the rallying cry in state legislatures across the country was "adult crime, adult time." Criminologists warned of the "superpredators;" those uber-violent juveniles without remorse who kill at will.

Juveniles can be sentenced to LWOP in 42 states. Fourteen states allow a minor to be tried as an adult at any age. Pennsylvania is one of those states and also leads the nation in juveniles serving LWOP. Pennsylvania has at least 330 offenders who were sentenced to LWOP as juveniles. Across the country more

## Youths Get Life in Prison in Thirty-one States

Judges in thirty-one states must sentence juveniles to life in prison without parole (LWOP) if they are convicted of first-degree murder or certain other offenses; judges in fourteen states have sentencing discretion. Five states and the District of Columbia do not permit juvenile LWOP. Pennsylvania has 444 youths serving life without parole—more than any other state.

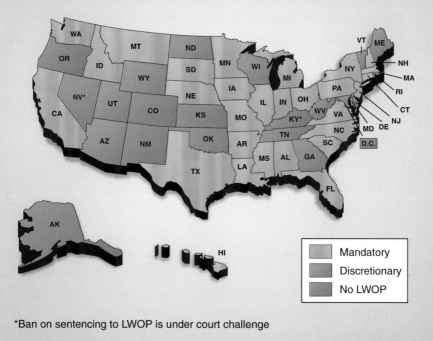

Mandatory
Discretionary
No LWOP

*Ban on sentencing to LWOP is under court challenge

Taken from: *CQ Researcher*, "Juvenile Justice," November 7, 2009. Source: "The Rest of Their Lives," Human Rights Watch, May 2008.

than 2,250 offenders are serving life sentences in adult prison for crimes committed as minors.

## A Changing Trend in Sentencing

When the U.S. Supreme Court made the landmark decisions in *Roper* as well as *Atkins v. Virginia*, banning the execution of the mentally retarded, the justices cited "evolving standards of decency." In the analysis of evolving standards of decency the court considers the acts of state lawmakers to establish a national consensus. When *Atkins* was argued, 30 states had banned the execution of the mentally retarded. When *Roper* was argued, 30 states had banned the execution of juveniles. Today, only eight states have banned LWOP for juveniles. In 2006, Colorado became the most recent state to repeal juvenile LWOP.

How did Pennsylvania become the nationwide leader in locking away juveniles for life? Following former Gov. Tom Ridge's special legislative session on crime in 1995, juvenile law changed dramatically. Most significant was the change in charging juveniles as adults. Prior to 1995, district attorneys had to request "certification" from the court to charge a juvenile as an adult. Today, district attorneys must charge a juvenile as an adult for specific offenses and the juvenile can request "decertification" to juvenile court.

## Most Life Sentences Not for Murder

According to the *Pittsburgh Post-Gazette* the number of juveniles committing murder nationwide dropped by nearly 55 percent between 1990 and 2000, yet the percentage of juveniles receiving LWOP increased by 216-percent. Fifty-nine percent of juveniles serving life had no previous criminal record and one in four were convicted of felony murder. The offender may have been a get-away driver, lookout or an accomplice in a robbery gone bad. Felony murder holds all offenders involved to the same level of responsibility as the primary perpetrator.

California has also been prodigious in imposing life sentences on juvenile offenders. A juvenile charged and convicted of murder as an adult with any of a long list of special circumstances can be sentenced to LWOP. There are currently 227 juveniles serving LWOP in California. California is considering a bill that would eliminate LWOP and limit juvenile sentences to 25 years to life. California is not alone. Illinois, Florida, Nebraska and Michigan are also considering similar legislation, a significant number but not exactly a national consensus.

## Multiple Sentencing Options Are Necessary

A case in Rhode Island points to the consequences of having inadequate options with regard to sentencing dangerous juvenile killers. In 1987, 13-year-old Craig Price murdered his neighbor. He stabbed her 58 times. Two years later, Craig stabbed and murdered Joan Heaton and her eight and 10-year-old daughters. At the time in Rhode Island children charged with a crime under 16-years-of-age could not be transferred to adult court.

Although Price nonchalantly confessed to the four murders he could not be held beyond the age of 21. Rhode Island had two juvenile lifers; both were over the age of 16 when they committed their offense. The law in Rhode Island has since been amended to address juveniles under the age of 16 who kill.

*The case of Craig Price, center, is an example of inadequate sentencing options for juveniles. Convicted of murder at thirteen, he killed three people two years later.*

Many involved in Price's prosecution argued that he was a dangerous serial killer and should be locked up for life. They fought to keep Price in prison where he remains today. The latest maneuver to keep Price in prison was a contempt of court sentence of 25 years for failure to submit to a court ordered psychiatric evaluation.

## A Disturbing Case

Lionel Tate was a 12-year-old Florida boy who, in 1999, was convicted of first-degree murder and sentenced to life in prison. Tate brutalized a 6-year-old girl, later arguing he accidentally caused her death while imitating wrestling moves. He spent five years in prison. In 2004, a Florida appellate court overturned his conviction on grounds that his competency had not been properly evaluated before his trial in 2001. He later pled guilty to second-degree murder and was sentenced to 10 years probation. He was released to his mother four days before his 17th birthday. According to the *New York Times*, Tate's lawyer said the teenager "posed no risk of flight or danger."

Within months Tate was cited for violating his probation. He was out after curfew and armed with a knife with an eight-inch blade. Fourteen months later, armed with a gun, Tate robbed a pizza deliveryman. He received a 30-year sentence for his latest probation violation. He recently pled guilty to armed robbery. With all the notoriety and the outcry for Tate's release, he could have ended up right where he started, and perhaps where he belongs, in prison for life.

## Life Sentences Should Be One Option

Abolishing juvenile LWOP eliminates an appropriate sentencing option in some cases. In Pennsylvania, LWOP for juveniles convicted of first-degree murder should be an option not a mandatory requirement.

Sentences, especially for juveniles sentenced as adults, should be specifically tailored for each individual offender.

Judges in Pennsylvania should have discretion to sentence juveniles to something other than LWOP following a conviction of first-degree murder. The idea in Pennsylvania that the juvenile lookout in a robbery gone badly should receive the same sentence as a juvenile serial killer doesn't make good sense or good law.

A juvenile sentenced to LWOP need not be doomed to a lifetime of hopelessness. The governor has the ability to grant clemency. Pennsylvania should follow the lead of Colorado and establish a juvenile clemency board. The board would be charged with the unique process of reviewing offenders who were sentenced to LWOP as juveniles. The legislature could establish parameters for consideration and guidelines for recommending clemency to the governor.

A solid approach to reconsidering LWOP for juvenile killers would include due consideration of public safety. This is not just a question of whether some violent juvenile offenders deserve to be locked away for life, but rather, do law abiding citizens deserve the protection that total incapacitation of dangerous offenders affords? Policy makers should not abolish LWOP without first deliberating the merits of judicial discretion and executive authority as appropriate corrective measures.

# TEN

# A Life Sentence Without Parole Is Not Appropriate for Juvenile Offenders

## Human Rights Watch

Human Rights Watch is an organization of international scope that upholds and defends human rights, gives a voice to the politically oppressed, and exposes the unjust and inhumane practices of their oppressors. This viewpoint draws attention to the growing practice of sentencing underaged criminal offenders to life in prison without parole—in the words of Human Rights Watch, tantamount to a capital offense—even though the world community finds such sentencing unacceptable. It addresses issues such as youths sentenced to life without parole (LWOP) who were not the violent offenders; the science which shows that the brains of juveniles are not developed enough to address in an adult manner the consequences of violent or risky behavior; racial disparity in sentencing; as well as the little-known fact that adults are often involved in crimes where teens are violent perpetrators—and the adults are usually given lighter sentences than the youths.

Approximately 227 youth have been sentenced to die in California's prisons. They have not been sentenced to death: the death penalty was found unconstitutional for juveniles by the United States Supreme Court in 2005. Instead, these young people have been sentenced to prison for the rest of their lives, with no opportunity for parole and no chance for release. Their crimes were committed when they were teenagers, yet they will die in prison. Remarkably, many of the adults who were codefendants and took part in their crimes received lower sentences and will one day be released from prison.

In the United States at least 2,380 people are serving life without parole for crimes they committed when they were under the age of 18. In the rest of the world, just seven people are known to be serving this sentence for crimes committed when they were juveniles. Although ten other countries have laws permitting life without parole, in practice most do not use the sentence for those under age 18. International law prohibits the use of life without parole for those who are not yet 18 years old. The United States is in violation of those laws and out of step with the rest of the world.

## Research on Youth Offenders

Human Rights Watch conducted research in California on the sentencing of youth offenders to life without parole. Our data includes records obtained from the California Department of Corrections and Rehabilitation and independent research using court and media sources. We conducted a survey that garnered 130 responses, more than half of all youth offenders serving life without parole in California. Finally, we conducted in-person interviews of about 10 percent of those serving life without parole for crimes committed as youth. We have basic information on every person serving the sentence in the state, and we have a range of additional information in over 170 of all known cases. This research paints a detailed picture of Californians serving life without parole for crimes committed as youth.

In California, the vast majority of those 17 years old and younger sentenced to life without the possibility of parole were

That's Life used with the permission of Mike Twohy and the Cartoonist Group.

convicted of murder. This general category for individuals' crimes, however, does not tell the whole story. It is likely that the average Californian believes this harsh sentence is reserved for the worst of the worst: the worst crimes committed by the most unredeemable criminals. This, however, is not always the case. Human Rights Watch's research in California and across the country has found that youth are sentenced to life without parole for a wide range of crimes and culpability. In 2005 Amnesty International and Human Rights Watch published a report showing that nationally 59 percent of youth sentenced to life without parole are first-time offenders, without a single juvenile court adjudication on their records.

## Not the Worst Crimes

In 2007, Human Rights Watch surveyed youth offenders serving life without parole in California. In 45 percent of cases surveyed, youth who had been sentenced to life without parole had not actually committed the murder. Cases include that of a youth who stood by the garage door as a look-out during a car theft, a youth who sat in the get-away car during a burglary, and a youth who participated in a robbery in which murder was not part of the plan. Forty-five percent of youth reported that they were held legally responsible for a murder committed by someone else. He or she may have participated in a felony, such as robbery, but had no idea a murder would happen. She or he may have aided and abetted a crime, but not been the trigger person. While they are criminally culpable, their actions certainly do not fall into the category of the worst crimes.

Murder is a horrible crime, causing a ripple-effect of pain and suffering well beyond that of the victim. Families, friends, and communities all suffer. The fact that the perpetrator is legally a child does nothing to alleviate the loss. But societies make decisions about what to weigh when determining culpability. California's law as it stands now fails to take into consideration a person's legal status as a child at the time of the crime. Those who cannot buy cigarettes or alcohol, sign a rental agreement, or vote are nevertheless considered culpable to the same degree as an adult when they commit certain crimes and face adult penalties. Many feel life without parole is the equivalent of a death sentence. "They said a kid can't get the death penalty, but life without, it's the same thing. I'm condemned . . . I don't understand the difference," said Robert D., now 32 years of age, serving a life without parole sentence for a crime he committed in high school. He participated in a robbery in which his codefendant unexpectedly shot the victim.

## Juvenile Brains Are Different

The California law permitting juveniles to be sentenced to life without parole for murder was enacted in 1990. Since that time, advances in neuroscience have found that adolescents and young adults continue to develop in ways particularly relevant to assessing criminal behavior and an individual's ability to be rehabilitated. Much of the focus on this relatively new discovery has been on teenagers' limited comprehension of risk and consequences, and the inability to act with adult-like volition. Just as important, however, is the conclusion that teens are still developing. These findings show that young offenders are particularly amenable to change and rehabilitation. For most teens, risk-taking and criminal behavior is fleeting; they cease with maturity. California's sentencing of youth to life without parole allows no chance for a young person to change and to prove that change has occurred.

## Racial Disparity

In California, it is not just the law itself that is out of step with international norms and scientific knowledge. The state's application of the law is also unjust. Eighty-five percent of youth sentenced to life without parole are people of color, with 75 percent of all cases in California being African American or Hispanic youth. African American youth are sentenced to life without parole at a rate that is 18.3 times the rate for whites. Hispanic youth in California are sentenced to life without parole at a rate that is five times the rate of white youth in the state.

California has the worst record in the country for racially disproportionate sentencing. In California, African American youth are sentenced to life without parole at rates that suggest unequal treatment before sentencing courts. This unequal treatment by sentencing courts cannot be explained only by white and African American youths' differential involvement in crime.

## Most Crime Committed Alongside an Adult

Significantly, many of these crimes are committed by youth under an adult's influence. Based on survey responses and other case information, we estimate that in nearly 70 percent of California cases, when juveniles committed their crime with codefendants, at least one of these codefendants was an adult. Acting under the influence and, in some cases, the direction of an adult, however, cannot be considered a mitigating factor by the sentencing judge in California. In fact, the opposite appears to be true. Juveniles with an adult codefendant are typically more harshly treated than the adult. In over half of the cases in which there was an adult codefendant, the adult received a lower sentence than the juvenile.

## Inadequate Legal Resources

Poor legal representation often compromises a just outcome in juvenile life without parole cases. Many interviewees told us

*Youths in a crowded California prison are shown here. Critics say that California's application of its juvenile statutes is outdated and discriminatory.*

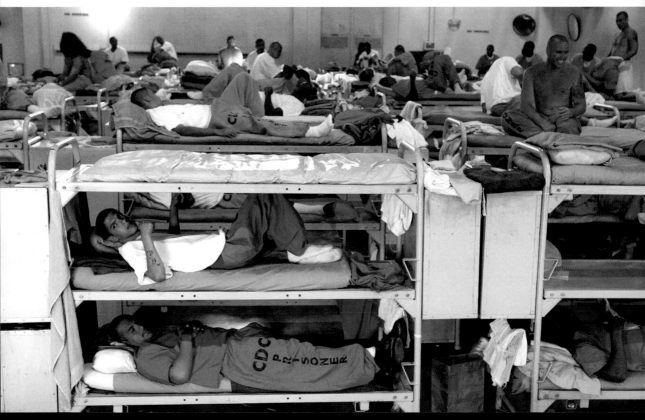

that they participated in their legal proceedings with little understanding of what was happening. "I didn't even know I got [life without parole] until I talked to my lawyer after the hearing," one young man said. Furthermore, in nearly half the California cases surveyed, respondents to Human Rights Watch reported that their own attorney did not ask the court for a lower sentence. In addition, attorneys failed to prepare youth for sentencing and did not tell them that a family member or other person could speak on their behalf at the sentencing hearing. In 68 percent of cases, the sentencing hearings proceeded with no witness speaking for the youth.

While some family members of victims support the sentence of life without parole for juveniles, the perspective of victims is not monolithic. Interviews with the families of victims who were murdered by teens show the complex and multi-faceted beliefs of those most deeply affected. Some families of victims believe that sentencing a young person to a sentence of life without parole is immoral.

## A Costly Endeavor

California's policy to lock up youth offenders for the rest of their lives comes with a significant financial cost: the current juvenile life without parole population will cost the state approximately half a billion dollars by the end of their lives. This population and the resulting costs will only grow as more youth are sentenced to spend the rest of their lives in prison.

California is not the only state that sentences youth to life without parole. Thirty-eight others apply the sentence as well. However, movement to change these laws is occurring across the country. Legislative efforts are pending in Florida, Illinois, and Michigan and there are grassroots movements in Iowa, Louisiana, Massachusetts, Nebraska, and Washington. Most recently, Colorado outlawed life without parole for children in 2006.

## Alternatives Exist

If life without parole for youth under age 18 were eliminated in California, other existing state law provides ample protection for public safety. California's next harshest penalty for murder secures a minimum of 25 years in prison. There are no reductions in the minimum time served for a murder conviction. Even then, parole is merely an option and won only through the prisoner's demonstrating rehabilitation. If they do earn release after 25 years or more, they are statistically unlikely to commit a new crime of any type. Prisoners released after serving a sentence for a murder have the lowest recidivism rate of all prisoners.

Public awareness about this issue has increased recently through newspaper and magazine articles and television coverage. With a significant number of the country's juvenile life without parole cases in its prisons, California has the opportunity to help lead the nation by taking immediate steps to change this unnecessarily harsh sentencing law.

# ELEVEN

# A Restorative Justice System Yields Positive Results

David J. Hines

Author David J. Hines is a retired police officer from the Woodbury, Minnesota, Police Department, with extensive experience working with the juvenile justice system and facilitating restorative justice programs. He points out that young people in the traditional justice system continue to maintain a disconnect between themselves—their own criminal actions—and their victims. Community service and/or sentences are understood as something to be endured, while the possibility of recidivism is not significantly reduced, says Hines. Restorative justice, which brings together the offender, the victim, and a third-party facilitator, allows the criminal better to understand the impact of the crime, gives a human face to all parties involved in the crime, and allows for a creative approach to making amends. Youth participating in such programs are significantly less likely to become repeat offenders.

There is a general consensus that juveniles involved in crime and delinquency should be handled differently than adults. Intuitively we have come to realize that juveniles' reasoning

David J. Hines, "Restoring Juvenile Justice," *GP Solo*, vol. 25. April/May 2008, p. 22. Copyright © 2008 American Bar Association. All rights reserved. Reprinted with permission. This information or any portion thereof may not be copied or disseminated in any form or by any means or stored in an electronic database or retrieval system without the express written consent of the American Bar Association.

powers are not yet developed to the same extent as adults'. Modern brain development research has proven that the part of the human brain responsible for judgment does not develop fully until about the age of 25. Crime statistics show that the majority of crime is committed by people between the ages of 15 and 25, with a secondary bump from 12 to 15. It behooves us, as a society, to intercede in these juvenile behaviors if we want to impact crime rates later in life.

## Juveniles in the Traditional Justice System

In most jurisdictions the current justice system separates juveniles from adults and seeks ways to impact juveniles' behavior so they will not continue to create harm in their communities. Judges assigned to juvenile court cases are reluctant to remove juveniles from the community until all other options are exhausted. It takes a concerted effort over a length of time for a juvenile to become institutionalized in most states.

The typical way of handling juveniles in our system is to impose sanctions on them that are meant both to punish bad behavior and teach better options in hopes of correcting that behavior. Juveniles involved in early moderate crime and delinquency are reprimanded and released in hopes they will self-correct, or they are assigned to rudimentary diversion programs where they are typically required to do some community service and write apology letters and sometimes a research paper. Often the community service is simplistic and routine, such as cleaning up the courthouse grounds, picking trash out of a roadside ditch, or sorting cans and bottles from the county's recycling bins. Although this work produces a real benefit to the public in some way, it generally has no real connection to the situation that brought the juvenile to this point.

Sanctions grow with the seriousness of behavior and the number of times a juvenile is seen in court. Eventually, juveniles will find themselves institutionalized but usually for a shorter time than for adults. Many states limit such detainments to anywhere from 90 days to six months, and it is rare for juveniles to receive more than a year in confinement unless they are remanded to adult court.

Juveniles who show emotional instability or the need for chemical dependency treatment are often court ordered to counseling and treatment programs, where the law allows. Unfortunately, the juvenile has no "buy in"—no personal investment in the treatment—and most often the programs fail to achieve behavior change. Certainly, most juveniles manage to stay clean for as long as urine tests are ordered, but as soon as the probation ends, the substance use resumes. Behavior contracts imposed by courts or probation often fail as well, especially when they require juveniles to achieve certain grades in school—the required level of scholastic success is often impossible for the juveniles.

The courts routinely order a range of probation sentences for juveniles. Informal probation, which is the kind most frequently ordered by the courts, requires a juvenile and guardian to have an initial meeting with a probation officer to receive instructions. The juveniles are then left to complete whatever is assigned them and will not see a probation agent again until the end, if ever. The mid-range of probation requires an agent to make telephone contact and in some cases at least one in-person contact during the duration of the probation period. Intensive probation, which is least frequently ordered by the courts, requires much more hands-on watching by the agent and may include electronic monitoring. In the usual understaffed and overextended probation offices, actual one-to-one work with any juvenile becomes very limited, if not impossible.

When necessary, the courts order placement outside the home. Usually this is done only if the juvenile has exhibited a long history of criminal and delinquent behavior largely uninterrupted by behavior change, or if the juvenile has committed actions that exhibit a blatant disregard for personal safety or a consistent threat to the safety of others. Options for placement range from community housing with day programs to state institutions in the prison system. The day programs are generally voluntary—they are not lockdown facilities and do not stop a juvenile from leaving.

Community placement programs have a multitiered system. First-timers are usually limited to a stay of no more than a couple days to two weeks. Juveniles who have shown more persistent behaviors can be assigned for 30-, 60-, and sometimes 90-day programs. These programs are outside the home but in the community, and they generally involve social services as well as probation services. Some community-based placements take the juvenile outside the community where they live.

Finally, there are programs within the state corrections system. Corrections-based programs range from "camp" programs to incarceration in juvenile prison settings. These are institutions that may offer more programming and education and counseling options than adult prisons but nevertheless are still surrounded by high walls, barbed wire fences, and electronic lockdown technologies. Camps look like any youth camp except for the fencing and warning signs on the perimeter of many. The camps have longer assignments ranging from 60 days to a year depending on jurisdictions. These programs include boot camps and are usually gender specific. Once the juveniles' assigned time is up, they return to the community, often with little or no preparation of those communities to receive these juveniles back into their midst.

Results of the typical system approach have not been very positive. Recidivism is high, with some juveniles believing that getting to the point of "doing time" is a badge of honor back in their community. Behavior change is rare, and generally we see an escalation of harmful behavior once the system begins assigning sanctions. Restitution is rarely received in full by victims, and some jurisdictions have all but stopped seeking it from juveniles.

## Restorative Justice and Juveniles

In light of these poor outcomes, an alternative system is gaining popularity in many parts of the United States and around the world. Restorative justice reverses some of the practices of traditional retributive justice while keeping many of its goals.

# Juvenile Courts May Impose a Form of Restorative Justice

Restorative justice is the means by which teen courts encourage juvenile criminals to take responsibility for their actions and to attempt to repair the harm caused by their crimes. Listed below are examples of restorative justice meted out by teen courts.

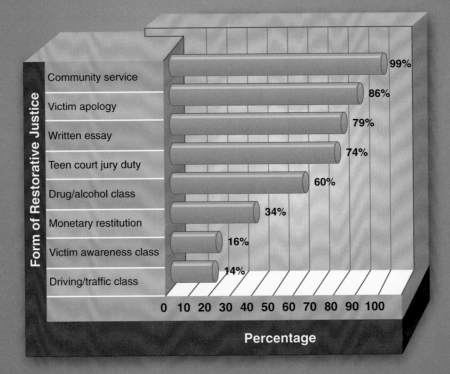

Taken from: John J. Wilson, "Teen Courts: A Focus on Research," *Office of Juvenile Justice and Delinquency Prevention Juvenile Justice Bulletin*, October 2000. www.ncjrs.gov.

Restorative justice seeks to protect the community by achieving real behavior change through building competencies, engaging the community and juvenile offenders in the process, and allowing victims to define the harm caused them and seek out adequate solutions to its repair through their direct involvement in the process. Restorative practices generally bring the offender, the victim, and the affected community together in a face-to-face meeting (or meetings) overseen by trained facilitators to discuss the incident and the behavior and seek solutions. The offender, the victim, and the community each has equal responsibility within the process, and solutions are achieved through consensus.

Restorative justice does not seek sanctions nor speak of punishment. In this approach, crime is viewed as harm to a person caused by another person, and the process seeks to repair that harm and impact future behavior. Juveniles in restorative justice are asked to recall their behavior, explore why they engaged in it, and find a way to repair the harm and improve their behavior for the future. Victims define the harm and explain what they need in terms of repair. Most importantly, they get to tell the offender how they felt and feel now because of the incident, and they do this face-to-face. The community can express how it is impacted and provide support to both victims and offenders as those offenders work to repair harm and change their behavior.

The whole process removes the case from the sterile, formal court environment to the community where the event occurred and those affected live. It is a process that begins as soon as the events are known and the participants identified. Because due process must be preserved and is as important to restorative justice as it is to the traditional system, this process is entirely voluntary, and it requires offenders to admit their involvement and be willing to seek a solution. Juveniles must have parental or guardian involvement and agreement to engage in this process if it is to go forward. Restorative practices do not argue guilt or engage in fact finding but assume basic factual agreement already exists. Where these issues are open, cases are referred to the traditional system, which is designed to deal with these issues and provides the best forum available to determine the facts of a case and assign guilt.

A typical restorative process begins with a facilitator studying the case and contacting key participants. The victim, juvenile and parents/guardians, and key individuals from the community are contacted, generally in that order. The process is explained, and all are told what will be expected of them in the process. Each person's story is heard, and each is "prepared" for the face-to-face meeting to come. All are encouraged to bring along some support person(s). At the face-to-face-meeting, each participant gets to tell his or her story, ask questions, and help decide the outcome. A consensus agreement ends the meeting. The facilitator is a neutral party who prepares the participants, facilitates the discussion, and writes out the agreement, but never decides or influences the outcome. Juveniles and parents/guardians participate directly, not through representation, and are free to end their participation at any time. Such a decision will put the case back into the traditional system.

## Typical Outcomes with Restorative Justice

Typically, cases where restitution is a factor see some form of restitution agreed to. Because the juvenile is actively participating and promising to pay, restitution is generally successful. Programs often see restitution repayment rates of 90 percent or higher. Consensus and victim participation help achieve this high rate by keeping the amounts reasonable and doable. Victims also often ask for symbolic or representative restitution in place of dollar-for-dollar payments. Sometimes juveniles will be asked to pay half in dollars and half in work such as helping set up a day care picnic event for the victim or helping to clean the victim's church. Juveniles tend to take this responsibility more seriously because they have promised to do it and were not told to or ordered to by a dispassionate or angry adult.

Where juveniles acknowledge chemical abuse or emotional distress, counseling and treatment are often part of an agreement. Once again, the success of this effort is more likely because the juvenile (and parents/guardians) have a "buy in" to the counseling. They are not being ordered to attend counseling; they are admitting the need and seeking the help. This is a significant difference and a recipe for success rather than failure.

Juveniles often agree to apologize for their actions, many times actively offering an apology. In these processes, apologies can be spoken directly to the victim and community in person. There is no need to write a letter, and apologies tend to be much more appreciated and heartfelt in this setting.

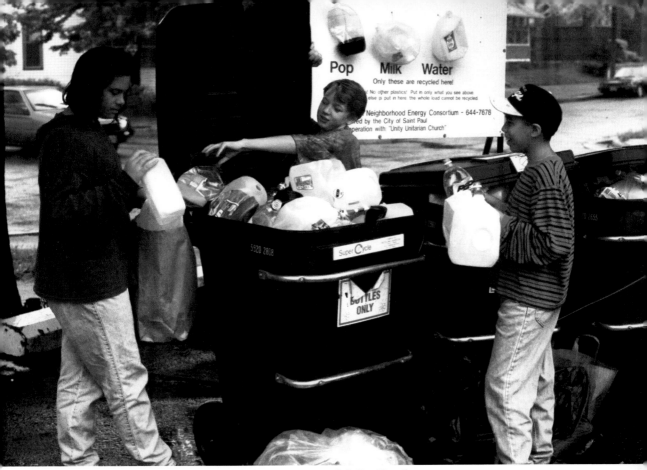

*In the restorative justice process, a youthful offender participates in an agreement designed to repair the harm his or her acts have caused. Community service can be an effective form of reparation.*

Community service is often part of an agreement. It tends to be more related to the act, or at least the juvenile better understands how this event has impacted the community and why he or she needs to make amends in a broader way. Many juveniles find they enjoy the work so much they seek ways to stay on and remain involved long after the required work is completed.

Agreements are tailored to each specific situation and are limited only by participants' imagination, local resources, and careful reality checking of each task. Community participants provide informal oversight and support the juvenile in the completion of the agreement.

Juveniles need to have timely intervention, and restorative practices can be done more quickly than the traditional system typically allows. When done as a diversion at the community level (i.e., when removed from the traditional system), cases can be brought to a meeting and an agreement can be in place within two or three weeks. The timeliness, sensibility, and flexibility of the agreements from these processes greatly enhance the success rates of restorative practices.

## Restorative Justice in the Traditional System

After working in the traditional system for nearly 30 years and practicing restorative justice for more than a dozen, I am convinced we need both. Not every case should be a restorative justice case, but not every case need be in the traditional system, either. The most crucial role the courts and its officers can play is timely referral of cases to restorative programs. As a police officer, I was able to immediately recognize and assign cases to restorative justice as they came in. Our agency cut the number of prosecution referrals in half and had better results, including a substantial reduction in recidivism and a drop in the overall juvenile crime rate thanks to proper use of both options. Local attorneys who knew of our program sometimes called me to suggest their client's case might better be dealt with by the community than the courts. Attorneys properly educated in restorative justice and its possibilities can and should make such recommendations. Although lawyers are not allowed to "practice" in a restorative setting, they can and do attend as supporters or community members. In my experience they are valuable assets in any restorative process.

Coordinators of restorative programming can be housed within the courts, the prosecutor's office, probation, or the police. They can help organize community volunteers, oversee cases, track agreements, and train facilitators and others in restorative justice. Such an arrangement helps facilitate timeliness and provides better tracking within the system.

Members of the traditional system—including judges, attorneys, probation, the police, and court administration—need to become educated in restorative justice. They need to understand the principles and practices at work, how to refer cases to local programs, what makes a good case for restorative justice, and which cases should not be referred. The traditional system has vast resources that can help any restorative justice program function more effectively, and the two systems must find ways to work together to increase the success of both. In the meantime, support from professionals within the traditional system for restorative justice and local initiatives is vital to providing the best service possible for the families, victims, and communities we serve.

# TWELVE

# Teen Courts Yield Positive Results

## Ritchie Eppink and Scott Peterson

Ritchie Eppink, an attorney with Idaho Legal Aid, and Scott Peterson, a program manager with the U.S. Department of Justice's Office of Juvenile Justice and Delinquency Prevention, present an alternative to the traditional juvenile court system that appears to be effective in reducing repeat offenses and is significantly less expensive than the traditional system: Youth Courts. Here teenagers serve as judges, lawyers, and jury members. Cases brought before Youth Courts are binding. Teenagers determine sentencing—often the length and scope of community service—and also invite the offender to participate in future court cases as a way of reconciliation and of welcoming them to participate in making the community a better place for everyone. For reasons as yet unknown, these courts show a high degree of success.

It is a simple idea that has inspired a grassroots movement and become the most replicated juvenile justice program in American history. In over 1,200 communities across the United States, in real criminal cases, youth volunteers are serving as the judges, juries, prosecutors, and defence counselors of their peers.

Both inexpensive and effective, these teen courts are community-based, volunteer-driven vehicles both for handling juvenile crime—several recent studies show that peer courts can significantly reduce recidivism—and for teaching teenagers about volunteerism, civic participation, and law.

## How Teen Court Works

Sarah, a fifteen-year-old growing up in the Town of Colonie, New York, gets caught stealing a purse full of cosmetics from a drugstore near her school. She is arrested and her parents are called to the police station. There, a juvenile services officer learns that Sarah has no prior arrests and, instead of sending her into the standard juvenile justice system, refers Sarah and her parents to the Colonie Youth Court, one of the country's most highly esteemed peer court programs.

An adult coordinator at the Colonie Youth Court meets with Sarah and her parents to confirm her eligibility for the teen court. Because Sarah is under sixteen and the theft is her first juvenile offence and a minor crime, she is eligible. The adult coordinator explains that before going any further, Sarah and her parents must all agree to refer her case to peer court—and Sarah must admit her guilt. By electing to proceed in the Colonie Youth Court, Sarah can avoid contact with the formal juvenile justice system, and like nearly all who are offered the teen court option, Sarah and her parents take it.

After signing paperwork to confess Sarah's guilt and consent to the teen court process, Sarah and her parents meet with her defender, Brandon. He is a teen Sarah's age who learns about her offence and background in order to prepare mitigating evidence and a sentencing recommendation for a jury of her peers. A teen prosecutor, Katy, also investigates Sarah and her crime and will represent the community's concerns before the youth court. Both Brandon and Katy, as well as the judge and the teen court clerk, are high school student volunteers trained by local volunteer lawyers. In the Colonie Youth Court's voluntary eight-week training course, about 120 youth each year receive

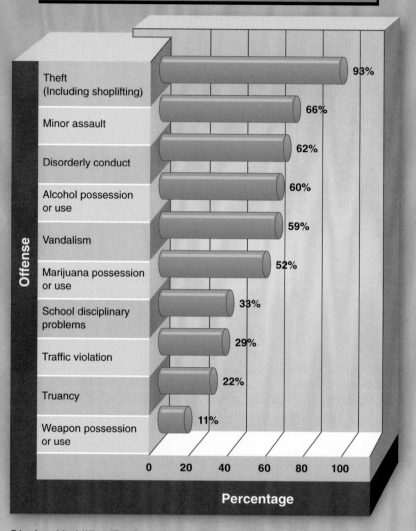

## Offenses Handled in Teen Courts

| Offense | Percentage |
|---------|-----------|
| Theft (Including shoplifting) | 93% |
| Minor assault | 66% |
| Disorderly conduct | 62% |
| Alcohol possession or use | 60% |
| Vandalism | 59% |
| Marijuana possession or use | 52% |
| School disciplinary problems | 33% |
| Traffic violation | 29% |
| Truancy | 22% |
| Weapon possession or use | 11% |

Taken from: John J. Wilson, "Teen Courts: A Focus on Research," *Office of Juvenile Justice and Delinquency Prevention Juvenile Justice Bulletin*, October 2000. www.ncjrs.gov.

an overview of the criminal and juvenile justice systems in New York, an appreciation for the causes of delinquency and the purposes of penal law, and an understanding of the goals of sentencing. Since completing the training, these volunteer students have been rotating through each of the teen court roles.

Once the youth prosecutor and defender have assembled their evidence and witnesses—including the police officer who arrested Sarah and the manager of the drugstore she stole from—Sarah's case goes before the Colonie Youth Court. The judge, robed and presiding with a gavel, is sixteen. A twelve-member youth jury hears the evidence too, and is made up of ten volunteers and two young offenders who are completing their own youth court sentence by serving as jurors in Sarah's case.

Katy, the prosecutor, and Sarah's defender, Brandon, each examine and cross-examine the witnesses and offer sentencing recommendations to the judge and jury. Katy argues that Sarah should pay $20 to the drugstore for the time its employees had to spend dealing with the theft, plus write an apology letter and work for fifty hours in the Colonie Youth Court community service program. Brandon points out that Sarah is a volunteer at her church and has already apologized in person to the store's manager. After a careful deliberation, the peer jury settles on thirty hours of community service and a two-page apology letter —a typical youth court sentence. The last two hours of Sarah's community service, as for every young offender sentenced in the Colonie Youth Court, must be filled by jury service on another youth's case in the court. When she completes her sentence, Sarah will get an invitation to come back and volunteer with the teen court. It was not her that the court did not like—just her behavior.

## Promising—but Unexplained—Success

Teen courts like the Colonie Youth Court have flourished in America. Since the idea caught on in the mid-nineties, the number of peer courts in the US has grown by over 1300%, from 78 in 1994 to more than 1,200 today. In 2005, American teen courts handled over 125,000 juvenile cases with the support of a staggering 110,000 youth volunteers.

With an average annual cost of under US $40,000 per year to run a teen court, it is not surprising that this youth justice program has attracted lots of attention. But it has been the measurable impact these courts are having that has transformed peer court from a simple idea into a nationwide grassroots movement. A recent multistate evaluation of teen courts compared young offenders processed by the regular juvenile justice system to offenders whose cases went to a peer court. The findings were remarkable: in one state, regular court offenders were two times as likely to reoffend as their peer court counterparts; in another, three times.

But just why teen courts work so well is not understood. The multistate evaluation authors confess "it is not exactly clear how teen court programs reduce recidivism." This means that it is hard for peer court coordinators to know which components of their programs to emphasize and develop. And figuring out the secret of the teen court model will be crucial as the movement's

*Youth courts such as this one in Wisconsin present alternatives to traditional justice. Teens serve as judges, lawyers, and jury members.*

rapid growth begins to draw criticism amongst the praise. Critics worry that young offenders who choose peer court over regular court are not making a choice at all. Will these youth —surrounded by fretting parents, facing the prospect of a permanent record, and without the counsel of a lawyer—sign just about anything an enthusiastic youth court coordinator puts in front of them? Peer court proponents will have to address this concern and explain why the concept works as well as it seems to.

## A Restorative Canadian Frontier?

Youth justice leaders in Canada have taken note of the peer court model's rampant success south of the border. Although no American-model teen courts have emerged in Canada so far, the efforts that are developing tend to be on the cutting edge, aimed with a holistic vision, and employing a restorative justice approach. Restorative justice is a turn away from the adversarial, punishment-oriented philosophy of criminal justice towards a focus on bringing victims, offenders, and the community together to repair harm, build understanding, and restore relationships.

While teen court coordinators in the States have been rethinking the peer court model as a restorative one for several years, in Canada, some program developers are eschewing the adversarial approach altogether in favor of purely restorative models. The Edmonton Youth Restorative Action Project is a federally sanctioned Youth Justice Committee made up entirely of youth between the ages of fifteen and twenty-four. Youth volunteers bring young offenders into roundtable discussions where they work together with victims, parents, police, psychologists, and others to discover resolutions for their offences and strategies for avoiding future harm. The project is in the process of replicating this restorative model in Ottawa and Toronto.

In Vancouver, Nora Gambioli, a program manager for the Law Courts Education Society of British Columbia, reports that studies of restorative practices with adults in BC "have consistently shown recidivism rates of 5%, and that recidivism in established school programs could be even lower, making restorative justice programs in schools a real total no-brainer" when applied in a school setting. The Law Courts Education Society's Peer Resolution Conferences for Youth program is an alternative to traditional school discipline procedures that brings young offenders, their victims, and their peers together to reach a consensus on meaningful and constructive consequences to restore community well-being. Programs like the Youth Restorative Action Project and this one are catching on in Canada and the US, and they may signal a restorative future for peer-oriented youth justice efforts in both countries.

## An International Movement

Wherever the peer court concept goes next, it will be a rapidly growing movement that takes it there. With the support of multiple federal agencies led by the Office of Juvenile Justice and Delinquency Prevention within the US Department of Justice, the Federal Youth Court Program has assumed a national coordinating role and invested millions of dollars in training events and resources for peer court volunteers. This summer [2007], local and state teen court leaders expect to incorporate a National Association of Youth Courts to facilitate skill-sharing. A comprehensive website, www.youthcourt.net, provides a clearinghouse for teen court information and research, and the US government will be releasing a twelve-year report on teen courts at an international peer court conference this December [2007].

There is little doubt that the movement will soon truly be an international one. American teen court programs continue to demonstrate phenomenal success, all at a miniscule cost. Peer courts not only appear to reduce repeat crime by youth, they are dynamic programs that promote volunteerism and community service, build a range of interpersonal skills in their participants, and interactively teach youth about law and justice in partnership with adults. Though letting youth co-operatively handle their own problems is a simple concept, it has turned out to be an uncommonly effective one—one that is fast becoming an integral part of youth justice in America.

# What You Should Know About Juvenile Crime

## The Prevalence of Juvenile Crime

According to the December 2009 *Juvenile Justice Bulletin* of the Office of Juvenile Justice and Delinquency Prevention:

- Sixteen percent of all violent crime arrests were juveniles.
- Twenty-six percent of all property crime arrests involved juveniles.
- Juveniles accounted for 12 percent of all violent crime convictions and 18 percent of all property crime convictions.
- Eleven percent of all murder victims in 2008 were under the age of eighteen, with one-third of those victims being under the age of five.
- Although African American youth aged ten to seventeen accounted for only 16 percent of the youth population in 2008, they accounted for more than half of the juvenile violent crime arrests for the year.
- The arrest rate in 2008 for robbery among youth was ten times higher for African Americans than for Caucasians.
- In 2008 there was a 3 percent decrease in overall youth crime from 2007, as well as a 2 percent decrease in violent crime perpetrated by youth.

## The Prevalence of Domestic Violence Perpetrated by Juveniles

The November 2008 *Juvenile Justice Bulletin* of the Office of Juvenile Justice and Delinquency Prevention focused attention on cases of domestic assault by juveniles:

- Two-thirds of all victims of juvenile domestic assault were female.
- Just over half of all juvenile domestic assault offenders attacked a parent; one-quarter of offenders attacked a sibling.
- Knives were most often used by juvenile offenders in cases of domestic assault.
- In cases of domestic assault, nearly 70 percent of juvenile offenders attacked someone over the age of eighteen; however, in cases of domestic sexual assault by juveniles, nearly all the victims were juveniles themselves.
- Females accounted for 35 percent of all juvenile domestic assault offenders.
- Most crimes of domestic assault perpetrated by juveniles were crimes in which the offender acted alone, and most of these crimes were committed in a home.
- Like adult offenders, juvenile assault offenders were less likely to be arrested in cases of domestic sexual assault than in cases of either aggravated assault or simple assault.

## The Prevalence of Sexual Victimization of Incarcerated Juveniles

According to the latest Bureau of Justice Statistics report (January 2010), during 2008 to 2009:
- Nine out of every ten young persons incarcerated in the United States were male.
- Twelve percent of all young people incarcerated in juvenile facilities reported one or more instances of sexual victimization —most (10 percent plus) involving facility staff.
- Just under half of the incidents between incarcerated youth and facility staff were described as forced encounters; the others were described as without coercion.
- Of the reports of staff sexual misconduct by youth in juvenile detention centers, 95 percent of the staff involved were female—although females account for just over 40 percent of employees in such centers.
- Gay, lesbian, bisexual, and transgendered (GLBT) youth experienced significantly higher rates of sexual victimiza-

tion than did heterosexual youth; 12.5 percent of GLBT youth reported victimization in comparison with just over 1 percent of heterosexual youth.

- Young people who had been sexually victimized before incarceration were more than twice as likely to report additional victimization while incarcerated; and one in five of these young people reported physical injuries in need of medical attention.
- Rates of staff sexual misconduct were higher in state-run facilities (nearly 11 percent) in comparison with facilities that were not run by states (less than 8 percent); while incidents of unwanted sexual advances by other young people were nearly identical in both types of facilities. As well, smaller facilities were less likely to see staff misconduct than were larger facilities.
- All-female facilities saw a higher rate of youth-on-youth sexual assault, while all-male facilities saw a higher incidence of staff sexual misconduct with incarcerated young people.

## The Prevalence of Juveniles as the Victims of Juvenile Violence

According to the Centers for Disease Control and Prevention (CDC), which also deals with violence prevention:

- In 2006 an average of sixteen young people a day were murdered in the United States.
- The second leading cause of death for young people in the United States is homicide.
- For African American youth, homicide is the leading cause of death.
- Nearly nine out of every ten homicide victims under the age of twenty-four are male.
- More than four out of five homicide victims under twenty-four are murdered with a firearm.
- Less than 1 percent of all homicides occur at school or on the way to or from school.

While less than 1 percent of homicides occur at school, the same CDC document on violence and youth reported:

- More than 35 percent of students surveyed nationally reported having been in a fight at school during the preceding year.
- Eighteen percent of those surveyed reported having carried a weapon to school at least once during the preceding month; males were more likely to carry weapons than were females—28 percent plus versus 7 percent plus for females.
- More than 5 percent of those surveyed carried a gun to school at least once during the preceding month.
- Nearly 8 percent of those surveyed reported having been threatened with a weapon during the preceding year.

# What You Should Do About Juvenile Crime

In 2007, 2.18 million people in the United States aged eighteen and under were arrested. You might know one, two, or several of these 2.18 million, or they might seem very far removed. In either case the problem of juvenile crime may seem both overwhelming and something that you cannot personally do anything about. However, there *are* some steps that you can take at your school and in your community that can make a difference in the lives of people behind the statistics.

## Become Involved at Your School

Crime and violence at school is a serious issue, but according to the Sacramento California County Sherriff's Department, students can play a significant role in preventing crime on their campuses in many ways.

First of all, you can be alert. If you encounter weapons, suspicious behavior or talk, or an actual crime, report it immediately to a teacher or counselor. You could also foster a culture of alertness at your school by starting a school crime watch, including a student patrol that could keep an eye on crowds, hallways, and parking lots and a system for students to report crimes anonymously.

You can also invest yourself in others. Notice new students and welcome them to your school. Set a goal to get to know at least one or two unfamiliar students every week. Mentor a younger student. As a friend and role model you can make it easier for a younger student to navigate the upper grades and make it through to graduation. Become a peer counselor if your school has a peer counseling program. If not, encourage your school to start one. All of these things can foster good relationships among students, reduce conflicts, and improve graduation rates, which can lower the chances of juvenile delinquency.

Finally, you can help develop a culture of peace and nonviolence at your school. Begin with yourself. Refuse to carry weapons, your own or others', or to keep quiet about the weapons of others. Learn about managing your own anger—how to talk and work things out or walk away without fighting. Be a peacemaker, helping others settle conflicts. Join a peer mediation program if your school has one or suggest that your school start one. Get your school to adopt a peace pledge initiative, asking students to promise to settle conflicts without violence and reject weapons. Set a goal of 100 percent student participation.

## Be a Friend

On a personal level there are ways that you can help prevent juvenile crime from ruining the life of a potential perpetrator. One of the risk factors for kids that get caught up in a life of juvenile crime is negative peer pressure, or the flip side, which is a lack of positive peer pressure. In the book *We Beat the Street: How a Friendship Pact Led to Success*, Sampson Davis, George Jenkins, and Rameck Hunt tell the true story of how, as teens in high school, they promised each other that they would not succumb to the streets of their rough Newark, New Jersey, neighborhood but would graduate from high school, go to college and medical school, and become doctors. They kept their promises, helping each other along the way—and themselves. Two are now doctors and one a dentist. Whether you live in a tough area like Newark or not, you need positive influences, and other students need positive influences, too. Set goals and be a friend, helping your friends—and new friends—set goals that will help keep them on track and away from crime as well.

Another risk factor for juvenile delinquency is not having supportive adults in your life. If you are lucky enough to have parents who do support you, you might consider sharing them with friends who do not. It does not have to be formal or obvious, although you should discuss it with your parents, explaining the situation, encouraging your parents to take an interest in your friend, and okaying it with them for your friend to spend plenty of time with your family.

## Read to Younger Children

According to the National State Boards of Education, one of every three juvenile offenders reads below the fourth-grade level, and about two of every three prison inmates are high school dropouts. With statistics like these, the value of volunteering as a reading tutor or simply reading to a child or listening to a child read to you cannot be undervalued. Look for a volunteer reading program at your school, at an after-school latchkey program, at your place of worship, or at your local library where you can read to younger children. If you cannot find a volunteer program, you may be able to talk one of these organizations into starting one, even an informal one, or you could work with a school or library and coordinate one yourself. As a young adult you can make a bigger impact on younger children than an older adult can, encouraging them to read and to value school—and making them feel important.

You could be the difference between the path toward a stable future and that toward a life of crime. Whether welcoming new people and helping them make new friends at your school, helping people solve conflicts at school before they escalate and someone is suspended, being a good friend, or just spending time with a younger child, there are many things you can do to help solve the problem of juvenile crime in your community.

# ORGANIZATIONS TO CONTACT

The editors have compiled the following list of organizations concerned with the issues debated in this book. The descriptions are derived from materials provided by the organizations. All have publications or information available for interested readers. The list was compiled on the date of publication of the present volume; names, addresses, phone and fax numbers, and e-mail and Internet addresses may change. Be aware that many organizations take several weeks or longer to respond to inquiries, so allow as much time as possible.

**ABA Juvenile Justice Committee**
740 Fifteenth St. NW, Washington, DC 20005
phone: (202) 662-1500
fax: (202) 662-1501
e-mail: juvjus@abanet.org
Web site: www.abanet.org/crimjust/juvjus/home.htm

An organization of the American Bar Association (ABA), the Juvenile Justice Committee disseminates information on juvenile justice systems across the country. The center provides leadership to state and local practitioners, bar associations, judges, youth workers, correctional agency staff, and policy makers. Its publications include the *Juvenile Justice Standards*, a twenty-four volume set of comprehensive juvenile justice standards; the report *More than Meets the Eye: Rethinking Assessment, Competency, and Sentencing for a Harsher Era of Juvenile Justice*; and the quarterly *Criminal Justice* magazine.

**American Academy of Child and Adolescent Psychiatry (AACAP)**
3615 Wisconsin Ave. NW, Washington, DC 20016-3007
phone: (202) 966-7300
fax: (202) 966-2891
e-mail: communications@aacap.org

Web site: www.aacap.org

The AACAP is a member-based professional organization composed of over seventy-five hundred child and adolescent psychiatrists and other interested physicians. It widely distributes information in an effort to assure proper treatment and access to services for children and adolescents. It publishes the parenting guides *Your Child* and *Your Adolescent*, fact sheets for families, informational videos, and a glossary of symptoms and mental illnesses.

**American Civil Liberties Union (ACLU)**
125 Broad St., New York, NY 10005
phone: (212) 549-2900
e-mail: www.aclu.org/general-feedback
Web site: www.aclu.org

The ACLU is a national organization that works to defend Americans' civil rights as guaranteed by the U.S. Constitution. It opposes curfew laws for juveniles and others and seeks to protect the public-assembly rights of gang members or people associated with gangs. Among the ACLU's numerous publications are the book *In Defense of American Liberties: A History of the ACLU*; the handbook *The Rights of Prisoners: A Comprehensive Guide to the Legal Rights of Prisoners Under Current Law*; and the briefing paper "Crime and Civil Liberties."

**American Youth Work Center (AYWC)**
1200 Seventeenth St. NW, 4th Fl., Washington, DC 20036
phone: (202) 785-0764
fax: (678) 387-0101
e-mail: info@youthtoday.org
Web site: www.aywc.org

The AYWC assists the staff and management of youth service organizations in the United States and abroad with the goal of improving services to children and youth. It advocates for increased funding for at-risk youth, offers training programs, and publishes youth work publications. The AYWC publishes the magazine *Youth Today: The Newspaper on Youth Work*.

**Boys Hope Girls Hope**
12120 Bridgeton Square Dr., Bridgeton, MO 63044-2607
phone: (314) 298-1250
fax: (314) 298-1251
e-mail: hope@bhgh.org
Web site: www.boyshopegirlshope.org

Boys Hope Girls Hope provides aid to families and youth. It offers counseling, education, and long-term housing to youth who wish to succeed but lack a supportive home life. The organization publishes the newsletter *Voice of HOPE*, which highlights the lives of successful alumni.

**Center on Juvenile and Criminal Justice (CJCJ)**
440 Ninth St., San Francisco, CA 94103
phone: (415) 621-5661
fax: (415) 621-5466
e-mail: dmacallair@cjcj.org
Web site: www.cjcj.org

The CJCJ was established to promote balanced and humane criminal justice policies that reduce incarceration and promote long-term public safety. The center's mission is pursued through the development of model programs, technical assistance, research/policy analysis, and public education. The organization offers many publications, including "Crime Rates and Youth Incarceration in Texas and California Compared: Public Safety or Public Waste?"

**Children Now**
1212 Broadway, 5th Fl., Oakland, CA 94612
phone: (510) 763-2444
fax: (510) 763-1974
e-mail: info@childrennow.org
Web site: www.childrennow.org

Children Now is a research and advocacy group that works on ensuring that children are the top public policy priority. The group focuses on health care, education, child care, and positive media for children. Children Now publishes the *California County Data Book*.

**Coalition for Juvenile Justice (CJJ)**
1710 Rhode Island Ave. NW, 10th Fl.
Washington, DC 20036
phone: (202) 467-0864
fax: (202) 887-0738
e-mail: info@juvjustice.org
Web site: www.juvjustice.org

The CJJ represents government-appointed juvenile justice advisory groups from the United States. The organization's goals include instituting reforms in the juvenile justice system, educating the public on juvenile justice issues, and aiding states in meeting the requirements of the Juvenile Justice and Delinquency Prevention Act. The CJJ provides a monthly newsletter on its Web site.

**Committee for Children**
568 First Ave. S., Ste. 600, Seattle, WA 98104
phone: (206) 343-1223
phone: (800) 634-4449
fax: (206) 343-1445
e-mail: info@cfchildren.org
Web site: www.cfchildren.org

The Committee for Children is an international organization that develops classroom curricula and videos as well as teacher, parent, and community training programs for the prevention of child abuse and youth violence. Second Step, the committee's violence-prevention curriculum, teaches children social skills and provides training for parents and teachers to practice and reinforce these skills with children. The committee publishes the newsletter *Second Step* four times a year and developed the programs Second Step, which teaches children how to change behaviors and attitudes that contribute to violence, and Steps to Respect, which focuses on bullying prevention.

### Fresh Lifelines for Youth (FLY)

120 W. Mission St., San Jose, CA 95110
phone: (408) 263-2630
e-mail: christa@flyprogram.org
Web site: www.flyprogram.org

FLY encourages teens in trouble to make healthy decisions by offering at-risk and disadvantaged youth education about the law, mentoring, and leadership training programs. The group advocates education, attention, and mentoring as the best ways to keep kids out of prison.

### The Heritage Foundation

214 Massachusetts Ave. NE, Washington, DC 20002
phone: (202) 546-4400
fax: (202) 546-8328
e-mail: info@heritage.org
Web site: www.heritage.org

The Heritage Foundation is a conservative public policy research institute. It advocates tougher sentences and the construction of more prisons as means to reduce crime. The foundation publishes policy papers on many issues, including crime, which are indexed and available online through their Web site.

### National Commission on Correctional Health Care (NCCHC)

1145 W. Diversey Pkwy., Chicago, IL 60614
phone: (773) 880-1460
fax: (773) 880-2424
e-mail: info@ncchc.org
Web site: www.ncchc.org

The mission of the NCCHC is to improve the quality of health care in jails, prisons, and juvenile confinement facilities. It offers accreditation, training, and seminars for correctional care health facilities; issues Standards for Health Services, which offers recommendations for improving medical and mental health care in correctional institutions; and publishes the journal *CorrectCare*.

**Office of Juvenile Justice and Delinquency Prevention (OJJDP)**
810 Seventh St. NW, Washington, DC 20531
phone: (202) 307-5911
fax: (202) 307-2093
e-mail: askjj@ncjrs.org
Web site: ojjdp.ncjrs.org

The OJJDP provides national leadership, coordination, and resources to prevent and respond to juvenile delinquency and victimization. The OJJDP supports states and communities in their efforts to develop and implement prevention and intervention programs and to improve the juvenile justice system so that it protects public safety, holds offenders accountable, and provides treatment and rehabilitative services tailored to the needs of juveniles and their families. The organization publishes the journal *Juvenile Justice*.

**The Pendulum Foundation**
5082 E. Hamden Ave., Ste. 192, Denver, CO 80222
phone: (720) 314-1402
e-mail: info@pendulumfoundation.com
Web site: www.pendulumfoundation.com

The Pendulum Foundation educates the public on child welfare and juvenile justice issues. It advocates on behalf of children, especially those in trouble with the law. The Web site offers testimonials, information, and resources on youth and issues of justice.

**Voices for America's Children**
1000 Vermont Ave. NW, Ste. 700, Washington, DC 20005
phone: (202) 289-0777
fax: (202) 289-0776

e-mail: voices@voices.org
Web site: www.voicesforamericaschildren.org

Voices for America's Children is a network of child advocacy groups. It seeks to maximize the effectiveness of such groups through the key policy goals of equity, health, school readiness, school success, safety, and economic stability. The Web site offers a database of publications on topics such as juvenile justice, child poverty and community mobilization.

**Youth Law Center (YLC)**
Children's Legal Protection Center, San Francisco, CA 94104
phone: (415) 543-3379
fax: (415) 956-9022
e-mail: info@youthlawcenter.com
Web site: www.ylc.org

The YLC is a public interest law firm that works to protect children in the nation's foster care and juvenile justice systems from abuse and neglect and to ensure that they receive the necessary support and services to become healthy and productive adults. The firm provides litigation, education, and advocacy on juvenile justice law. The YLC's Web site offers fact sheets on a variety of issues concerning child welfare and juvenile justice.

## BIBLIOGRAPHY

### Books

John Aarons, Lisa Smith, and Linda Wagner, *Dispatches from Juvenile Hall: Fixing a Failing System*. New York: Penguin, 2009.

Sampson Davis, George Jenkins, Rameck Hunt, and Sharon Drapers, *We Beat the Streets: How a Friendship Pact Led to Success*. New York: Puffin, 2006.

Laura Bufano Edge, *Locked Up: A History of the U.S. Prison System*. Minneapolis: Twenty-first Century, 2009.

Jean Otto Ford and Celeste Carmichael, *Rural Crime and Poverty: Violence, Drugs, and Other Issues*. Broomall, PA: Mason Crest, 2008.

Debbie J. Goodman and Ron Grimming, *Juvenile Justice: A Collection of True Crime Cases*. Upper Saddle River, NJ: Prentice-Hall, 2007.

John Hubner, *Last Chance in Texas: The Redemption of Criminal Youth*. New York: Random House, 2008.

Susan Kuklin, *No Choirboy: Murder, Violence, and Teenagers on Death Row*. New York: Holt, 2008.

Mark Salzman, *True Notebooks: A Writer's Year at Juvenile Hall*. New York: Vintage, 2004.

Elizabeth S. Scott and Laurence Steinberg, *Rethinking Juvenile Justice*. Cambridge, MA: Harvard University Press, 2008.

Seventeen Magazine, *Seventeen Real Girls, Real-Life Stories: True Crime*. New York: Hearst, 2007.

Sandra Simkins, *When Kids Get Arrested: What Every Adult Should Know*. New Brunswick, NJ: Rutgers University Press, 2009.

### Periodicals

Robert H. Bork, "Travesty Time, Again: In Its Death-Penalty Decision, the Supreme Court Hits a New Low," *National Review*, March 28, 2005.

*Christian Century*, "Ruling to Ban Minors' Executions Is Praised," March 22, 2005.

*Community Care*, "Early Warning," August 5, 2004.

Patrick Griffin and Mary Hunninen, "Preparing Youth for Productive Futures," *Pennsylvania Progress*, 2008.

Ron Honberg and Darcy Gruttadard, "Flawed Mental Health Policies and the Tragedy of Criminalization," *Corrections Today*, February 2005.

Lise Olsen, "Certified as Adults, but Still Children. Harris County Has an 'Assembly Line' for Juvenile Justice, Critics Say," *Houston Chronicle*, June 7, 2009.

Sarah S. Pearson, "What's Behind Youth Courts' Growth Spurt?" *State News*, September 2004.

Scott Bernard Peterson, "Made in America: The Global Youth Justice Movement," *Reclaiming Children and Youth*, Summer 2009.

Lisa Poliak, "Teen Crime Adult Time," *Junior Scholastic*, January 24, 2005.

Florencio Ramirez, "Juvenile Delinquency: Current Issues, Best Practices, and Promising Approaches," *GP Solo*, April/May 2008.

Paula Schaefer, "Girls in the Juvenile Justice System," *GP Solo*, April/May 2008.

Christine Siegfried, "Victimization and Youth Violence," *Prevention Researcher*, February 2007.

Howard N. Snyder, "Juvenile Arrests 2006," *OJJDP Fact Sheet*, November 2008.

Howard N. Snyder and Carl McCurley, "Domestic Assaults by Juvenile Offenders," *Juvenile Justice Bulletin*, November 2008.

Anne L. Stahl, "Delinquency Cases in Juvenile Courts, 2004," *OJJDP Fact Sheet*, February 2008.

Susanna Zawacki, Patricia Torbet, and Patrick Griffin, "Addressing the Behavioral Health Needs of Court-Involved Youth," *Pennsylvania Progress*, 2008.

Mangino, Matthew T., 75
Mara Salvatrucha, 28
McFadden, Martin, 22–23
McGrath, Michael, 23–24, 25, 26
Mental health problems
  treatment of, deficiencies in
    juvenile detention centers,
    63–65, 69
Monitoring the Future study,
  36
Moore, Joan, 31
Multi-systemic therapy
  (MST), 69–71
  use of by Rural Appalachia
    Project, 72–74
Murder/murder rates, 11
  juveniles charged as adults
    for, 57
  in major cities, *20*
  percent involving juveniles,
    10, 11–12

N
National Crime Victimization
  Survey (Bureau of Justice
  Statistics), 36
National Longitudinal Study
  of Adolescent Health, 39–40
National Survey of
  Adolescents, 44, 45
New York City schools,
  police/school safety officers
  in, 5–6
*New York Times* (newspaper),
  76, 80
Nutter, Michael, 21, 23

O
Office of Juvenile Justice and
  Delinquency Prevention
  (OJJDP), 9, 33, 106
*Ohio, Terry v.* (1968), 22
O'Malley, Martin, 58

P
Peterson, Scott, 100
Physical/sexual abuse
  percent of youth
    experiencing, 44, *44*
*Pittsburgh Post-Gazette*
  (newspaper), 78
Police officers, in New York
  City schools, 5–6
Population, juvenile
  percent with mental/
    emotional disorder, 69
  racial composition of,
    16–17
Post-traumatic stress disorder
  (PTSD), 45–46
Price, Craig, 79, *79*–80
Property crime
  ethnic differences in arrest
    rates for, 17
  by female gang members, 30
  gender differences in decline
    in, 16
  juvenile arrests for, 15
  percent involving juveniles,
    10, 12–13
Prowse, Cathy, 28
Puberty, as factor in girls' risk
  for delinquency, 38
Puzzanchera, Charles, 9